CHILD SEXUAL ABUSE

Never Call It "Love!"

By

Deirdre McNamara

A Celtic Balm LLC Publication

www.drdmcn.wix.com/celticbalm

Copyright 2015 Dr. Deirdre McNamara.

All rights reserved.

"Child Sexual Abuse" is an expanded response to the 2005 Irish Bishops' "Lenten Reflection on Child Sexual Abuse"

Deirdre McNamara is a Doctor of Homeopathy and Substance Abuse Minister certified by the Archdiocese of New York with further studies in Spirituality and Substance Abuse at the International Center for the Disabled in New York City.

She was Homeopath to the Missionaries of Charity in NY. In Ireland, she treated recovering addicts with Hepatitis C among other problems. Hahnemannian Homeopathy's success rate was 100%! All patients free and clear of viral load.

Homoeopathy's thorough anamnesis allowed patients to reveal underlying grief and trauma and provided a sad but powerful insight into the long term effects of Child Sexual Abuse such as alcoholism, self-harm and other addictions.

NEVER CALL IT 'LOVE' is dedicated to those most in need and most deserving of Love – the world's precious and beloved little children, including those awaiting birth.

"And whoever welcomes a little child like this in my name welcomes me. But if anyone causes one of these little ones who believe in me to sin, it would be better for him to have a large millstone hung around his neck and to be drowned in the depths of the sea...for his angel always sees the face of his Father in Heaven"

Jesus' own words from Matthew. 18:5-6

INTRODUCTION

Statistics offered in the Irish Bishops' Lenten Reflection, "Toward Healing," state that one in four men and one in three women have survived child sexual abuse.

Anecdotally, the actual numbers are twice as high, and given the low rate of reporting in the sexual abuse of children and/or violence against adults, male and female, the anecdotal evidence triumphs.

Denial is a strong ally in the survival process. The mind and endocrinal system shut down or provide multiple diversions and strategies to allow daily functioning to continue. Prolonged, of course, it can lead to mental or physical illness, substance abuse, dysfunction, depression, spousal abuse, child abuse, sex crimes and suicide.

In compiling statistics, it is important to agree on definitions.

It is also important to call it what it is: a PHOBIA, not a 'PHILIA.'

"Love" brotherly or otherwise has as much to do with Child Sexual Abuse as it has to do with the rape of an adult.

Psychiatry's perpetuation of this myth has enabled not just the paedo-perv, but an entire industry of "specialists' in this "tragic, misguided" "attraction" to children.

Child Sexual Abuse is perpetuated by persons with a visceral HATRED of children; hatred of their beauty, innocence, sweetness and vulnerability.

Because it is a constant reminder that their beauty, vulnerability and innocence was seized by a monster similar to the one that they have now become.

While the inclusion of Catholic clergy in the lists of Child Abusers is a wound to all Catholics, scapegoating the clergy has only served to distract from the real nature and pathology of the grossly misterm Paedo 'philia' and allowed Child Sexual Abusers to organize and extend their vile and destructive practices to an incomparable and unimagineable degree.

I hope to shed some light on why most victims of Child Sexual Abuse become protective of other children and go on to live normal lives while others become predators themselves.

CHAPTER ONE

Background

Sustained and ongoing sexual abuse of a vulnerable, unprotected child will have a greater impact than the brief, opportunistic molestation of a boy or girl in a movie house or classroom. Victims of extreme, sadistic, homicidal pedophiles seldom survive, childhood, and if they do, seldom make it to 'retirement.'

Those bereaved by such crimes are victims too, and need maximum support and whatever comfort can be both provided to and accepted by them.

In all cases of CSA, irrespective of degrees of severity, the "shell" has been broken: the child's sense of safety and autonomy shattered; the right to control his/her body and senses destroyed. Premature sexual awakening can alter relationships with peers or family – even other children.

The world has been transformed. It is no longer a place of innocence, trust and freedom; it is now a place of darkness and predation. And the child will never feel safe again; and the personality remains dis-integrated, unwhole, but not always visible to others. Many victims conceal their suffering in good works or protecting others, professionally or socially.

The Adult is no longer trustworthy and benevolent. The parent figures lose their omnipotence. In the victim's sensibility, the parent has failed to protect him or her, and in the child's reasoning, whether the parent is present or not, the parent is complicit. The omniscient should have known, seen the warning signs, etc, but few children can identify or articulate the flood of emotions and sense of betrayal that follow child sexual abuse – instead lashing with anger and 'inappropriate' behavior.

A feisty young boy who can retaliate with a kick to the shins or a contemptuous remark may still carry scars and find difficulty in admitting the encounter, even in adulthood, but it will not destroy him.

For a child subjected to continuous, sadistic abuse in institutions, healing will be painful, prolonged, almost impossible. Therapists and counselors of such survivors require special selection, training and support as memories are uncovered, rage displaced, hostile transferences occur.

More than counselors and therapists, the child will need love and assurance.

"It is better a millstone be hung around his neck and he be drowned than he scandalize a child..."

Christ, understanding and forgiving of human sexual frailty, drew a very different line in the ground between human weakness and child sexual abuse.

Somewhere, our anger toward the Church for failing to understand the nature of predatory pedophilia and laicise sacerdotal offenders comes from a sense that the Church *abdicated* her role as guardian of morals and protector of the Faithful, and ceded 2015 years of the Counsels of the Holy Spirit to the followers of an unethical, coke-addled, phallocentric, sex addict and plagiarist named Sigmund Freud.

Shockingly, the same acquiescence is occurring with islam.

Do our Church leaders do their homework, or is Christ just not 'good enough' anymore?

CHAPTER TWO

Reactions and Responses

Shame and self-blame shadow survivors. This facilitates their predators, who work on their fear and weakness, using a confusing combination of threats, bribes, bullying, stalking, intimidation and ridicule, to undermine the child's self-worth and integrity.

It is now understood that children must be given permission to defend themselves from sexual abuse: That adult privileges and 'respect' do not extend to the right to molest children and commit horrendous crimes against them.

In fact, at a suitable age, children can be taught that _any level of self-defense is appropriate and necessary._

Response to a child's report of sexual abuse, and the gathering of evidence must be handled very carefully so that a child does not feel:

> Responsible for his/her victimization

> Frightened of consequences for himself and parent.

A parent's understandable and reflexive rage toward the perpetrator can discourage an already *traumatized child from providing information that would indict and help to convict his/her assailant.*

Best to take a few deep breaths before responding calmly and reassuring the child that s/he is not responsible for the crime or harm from which s/he has suffered so grievously.

Hug and assure the child. Allow him/her to continue at his/her own pace. *Do not rush or pressure your child.* S/he has had enough of that from the predator. Do offer breaks.

It is likely that the little one will be so relieved at the new freedom to communicate his/her suffering that s/he will want to keep going. Watch however, for mental fatigue, stumbling over words, etc., and ensure that s/he is nourished and hydrated. And appropriately hugged.

Predators are notorious for threatening parents, and victims often believe that their silence protects their parents from murder and death, a fear the pedo-pervs play on.

Socially isolated and marginalized.

The child victim must be allowed to work through his/her trauma in a safe environment and *be allowed* to move on when ready. Parental guilt and neuroses must not be allowed to interfere with the child's recovery.

While the focus must be on the victim, assistance or counseling of parents is an essential adjunct to the recovery of the child's mental health and equilibrium.

In a detached, 'sane,' professional world, it is not always easy to imagine an over-worked, sleep-deprived, guilt-ridden parent suddenly lashing out at a child with the words:

"How could you do this to *me!*"

But it happens.

It's analogous to a mother pulling a child out of immediate danger and then 'smacking' him or her in an unreasoned mix of fear, terror and relief.

Video surfaced of the interrogation of a little boy named 'Gabriel' by British police in Hampstead, London. He was a remarkable young fellow, brave, intelligent, honest, but the cop treated him like a shifty retired barrister or highly trained Special Ops captive.

Instead of taking the boy's testimony, and investigating it, and/or putting it in the context of a child's perception, the cop constantly challenged him, asked the same questions repeatedly, tried to confuse him, ignored rather scary statements, and made him re-iterate over and over testimony that was highly personal and painful. This video should never have made it to You Tube, and it is quite probably a source of delight to those who would hurt children.

The tactics used also give credence to multiple rumors of high level child sexual abuse and trafficking rings.

Certainly the number of Labor MPS arrested during Blair and Brown's tenures as Prime Minister, along with a number of pervs on the other side of the Parliamentary tables suggest that the odious and malignant child abuse gangsters are well protected in England, Ireland, the USA.

No such protections are required in the Middle East where followers of the child rapist, Mohammed have unfettered access to children, both male and female. For the purposes of adult abusers, boys are considered female until puberty.

Young Gabriel was bullied into retracting his statement which involved a large number of people in Hampstead. I believe you, Gabriel, and it's *not your fault* that you were intimidated into changing your story,

The fact that hallucinogenics were given to him and other children in order distort their perceptions and discredit you as witnesses provides more disturbing evidence that, influenced by Islamic invaders, England is turning into a moral swamp.

Gabriel - you're just a kid, and a brave little one at that!

Justice will be done.

CHAPTER THREE

Consequences of CSA

The irony of CSA may be that the very systems used by the human body to protect itself from trauma and disease during procreative (sexual) activity can set the victim up for a life of inner torment, sometimes displaced outward in the perpetuation of abuse.

The body's natural response to procreation with a spouse is one of pleasurable sensation and a set of physiological reactions known collectively as "arousal."

These reactions include the release of epeniphrene and endorphins into the system, increasing the heart and respiration rates and inducing a state of "aggression" or ardency in the male and euphoria, sometimes "passivity" in the female. Dilation and lubrication of sensitive tissue protect and assist the human procreative process to continue without pain or damage to person or mind.

In other words, an endocrinal (hormonal) bouillabaisse starts simmering away with the design of providing a happy experience that the couple will repeat in the hope of pro-creating more happy little humans.

On such a system, or intelligent design, rests the survival of the human race. It's a strong, enduring system, far more complex than in the animal kingdom, and where humans are concerned, is also fraught with fragilities and vulnerabilities. And that's in *normal, consenting, spousal* relationships.

And now, *send in the pervs.*

And no, I won't call them "pedo" or "paedo" "*philes!*" Because *Philia*, ie, brotherly love, has no say in this horror. Paedoperv is more accurate, reflecting a perverted interest in sexualing, seducing, hurting, raping, or otherwise harming a child.

It's politically incorrect and professionally discourteous to pin authentic or descriptive labels on frightening or criminal conditions in this wearying times.

In a warped, post Freudian, post drugs and libertine era, if it "feels good," it *is* good.

And don't the paedo-pervs all feel good at the expense of our children...

I doubt it. In the early stages they feel a profound level of disgust and self-hatred.

Which they relieve by despoiling another innocent. The addict relieves his/her remorse by repeating the act that caused it in the first place! That's why they call it: "addiction," human kinds only self-perpetuating condition or syndrome. Most genetic impairments self heal by the third generation.

"It was done to me. So I'm going to get back at the society that failed to protect me by hurting as many other children as possible."

"I may also revisit my innocence, or who I was at that age...but I know I'll never regain my innocence, my normal sexuality. I'll start to convince myself that this is normal, the ultimate "love" as in NAMBLA (America's powerful North American Man Boy Love Association, similar to Britain's "PIE" or Pedo-perv Information Exchange.) *I'll cultivate other 'pervs' and we'll convince one another with the help of equally sick elements in the media, that the children want us, that the children COME ON TO US!"*

How sick is that!

So sick that they believe it.

Along with other non-reproductive sexual preferences or deviations, Child Sexual Abusers are made, not born. In thirty years of work in the Arts and alternative medicine, I have yet to meet a homosexual or CSA who was *not* molested in childhood or early adolescence. On the other hand, there is a high incidence of physical abuse by a male family member or friend in lesbians.

Many heterosexuals were molested in childhood, and still retained their sexual identity, with the right help and environment or at considerable personal or financial cost to self or family.

As with child victims of domestic violence or battery, a very small proportion of whom will go on to perpetuate violence against their own children, early childhood molestation does not turn every child, or even most children into a paedo-perv; but it will turn some. It will however, cause: extreme distress, sudden tears, tantrums, nightmares, fire-lighting, match lighting, insecurity, clinging, soiling, and other such behaviors baffling to the loving and frightened parent.

The outcome rests heavily on so many factors:

1. Age of molestation

2. Type of molestation, eg, violent, touching, invasive, seductive, coercive

3. Relationship with molester – eg family, friend, professional or stranger

4. Duration of molestation

5. Repetitive or single act

6. Temperament of child – they choose shy children whenever possible, avoid assertive children

7. Relationship with parent

8. Stability in home life

9. Availability of trusted person to listen and identify

a. Reaction of trusted person to the child's
      testimony.

Paedo-pervs are made, not born that way.

Honest, ethical, careful studies are urgently needed
to determine at which age the personality diverges
into identification with the molester, and which
factors determine the victim/survivor's ultimate
destiny.

My money is on a trusted confidante, especially a
parent.

Moms and Dads – don't yell at your child for
muddying her dress, or tearing his pants: look into
their eyes first, make sure that they are well – *every
single time they come in from school.*

CHAPTER FOUR

Challenges for Professionals

Meet the victims! Meet the perps!

"Vic 1" was molested at age 12. He is heterosexual, promiscuous, unable to engage in an adult or committed way with women, but has continuing and disturbing fantasies about engaging in homosexual activities with others. Fondling only.

He finds that frightening and directs his drives to uncommitted relationships with women – exploitation – and auto eroticism.

Auto eroticism is not always 'victimless.' Ask any survivor of a stalker who can no longer differentiate between sexual fantasies and reality.

The stalker has to be understood in a different light to the "moonish youth" haunting his "beloved."

The stalker wants to "own," become and replace the victim. He/she does that by controlling and destroying the victim's life. It's virtual murder. And sometimes leads to murder.

The preferred porn of such parties is filled with domineering and sadistic images.

He seeks to regain the control lost in childhood to another malevolent, and to malignantly metastasize his suffering to others.

The Act of Pro-creation is ordered toward team-work, cohesion, mutual care, love and protection in the interest of offspring and future generations. It is a gift but comes with responsibility – a responsibility mocked and abdicated by the 'Peace and Love" and exploitation generation, with terrible consequences for children, and inevitably, their grandchildren.

Pedo 'philes' are now highly organized, and children are at risk in almost every public area.

"Vic 2" is in his twenties. Appears younger. Sad, victim like appearance. Prowls religious communities, speaking in hushed, sanctimonious tones about his "vocation." Due to his association with respected religious communities, his credibility is high and wealthy American Catholics offer him scholarships to seminaries and trips to the Vatican.

His purpose in life is access to young Hispanic boys. He states this with an air of triumphalism.

"What are you going to do about it! You can't stop me!" is the subtext...

"Vic 2" was incested by his own father at a very young age. This was allegedly repeated. "Vic 2" sought to reclaim power and autonomy through occult practices, like signing his soul away, but claims to have renounced such practices after a "conversion."

Characteristic of the "victim" he compromises the professionals who try to help him. He lets us know his intent and enjoys our powerlessness.

He gives us "intent," but no evidence. Everything to fear on behalf of the children with whom he volunteers, but nothing concrete to report to Child Welfare authorities, despite laws obliging professionals to report incidents of child molestation. We cannot report generalized 'intent' to the authorities, only a specific threat.

A Canon lawyer advised me of a moral obligation to advise the religious communities of this young man's subversive interests. He is still allowed to participate in programs. I, however, became *non grata* in that highly respected community.

I am haunted by another case. Again, no concrete evidence to report, just intuition and the behavior of child and father.

Little "Vic 3" was two and a half. She came in with her father, a morose, hostile American, married to a European women whom I never met and who always "too busy" to accompany her child. "Vic 3's" father was in his thirties, a professional, well-featured but with a cold and unpleasant manner.

He was at great pains to insist that he could only bring the child on Saturday when my receptionist would be off-duty and I had to make an exclusive trip to go into the city and open up.

Dr. McNamara was expected to make sacrifices for a child that the parents were unwilling to make, but I did so.

Seldom in my practice do I fail to win the trust of a child! Never have I had to work so hard!

Little "Vic 3" was subject to multiple Urinary Tract Infections. (UTIs) She had been seen by many paediatricians, but they were "useless" and "incompetent" and her father would not give me their names for conference, nor provide official medical history.

Multiple UTIs in children are one flag in suspected child molestations if other factors are in place.

The second flag was the number of dismissed paediatricians. Doctor-hopping is an oft used strategy to prevent the build-up of date, history, potential evidence sharing. It can also indicate a genuinely over-anxious parent, or other problems, so best not rush to judgment on that basis alone.

The third flag was the number of layers of clothing on the child on a warm day, making it difficult to remove them for examination.

The fourth, and most poignant, was her sad, withdrawn personality. "Vic 3" was in her own world, afraid of touch or approach – indicators of trauma – but she obeyed her father mechanically when he called her over. No "terrible two's there. A tantrum would have been far preferable to the bleakness of the little girl's affect.

Without consideration of the other factors, this little one would probably be diagnosed as an "Aspergers" child.

I prescribed according to the symptoms provided by her father and by objective perception of the fragility and withdrawn personality of the sweet little girl.

By the second visit she was showing some improvement, and while she did not permit me to examine her – withdrawing at the mere idea of removing any garment, she did allow me to gently remove and replace her hat.

This did not please her sour father. He said he'd forgotten his checkbook, would send a check. When I called a month later regarding the latter, he accused me of "indifference" to his child, and said that he would not be returning to my practice, despite manifest improvement in her condition.

Some "indifference!" Opening my office on a Saturday morning for one little patient.

It appears that I had come too close, and I suspect that he was afraid that "Alice" would eventually trust me enough to let me examine her, and he didn't want me to see evidence of trauma in her defenseless little body.

If I trusted the NY authorities, I might have taken a chance in discussing this with them, but the NYC child welfare agency is the most mismanaged bureaucracy in Manhattan, and I already had experience of their incompetence and inefficiency in *specific* cases where accusations had been made and were subsequently proven to be founded, but dismissed by NYC CPS.

One of the saddest victims of paedo rape was the well-known homosexual advocate, the late Quentin Crisp, who wondered in his book, if there were redemption for such as he. (His "non PC" comments are edited out of later editions)

Quentin was molested by an actor visiting his school. An isolated child, with sad, depressed and indifferent parents, he was overwhelmed by the attention and charm showered upon him by the predator. Later, he read that the actor in question had been punished for his act of predation, and seems, from then, to have decided to become an overt advocate for homosexuals.

In other words, *Quentin took on the role of protector of* his molestor. The predator had chosen his victim well, the shy, withdrawn child lacking in confidence, grateful for any acknowledgment or kindness. The predator had spoken kindly to him, selected him out of all the boys for special attentions, invited him to his dressing room, gave his lonely little life a certain 'cachet' or 'glamor,' and as the young Quentin was too young to understand the long term consequences of the predator's actions, he bonded and identified with his predator.

Quentin Crisp's description of bleak, subjugated lower-mid English family life gives his reactions a deep poignancy.

In early editions of "The Naked Civil Servant," Crisp writes of the difference between homosexual and heterosexual relationships.

I have searched for those quotes in current editions, but they appear to have been expunged. They were honest words and may have caused his ostracisation from militant, political homosexuals in New York.

Hence his lonely seat at a lonely table in a new Night Club in NYC.

I did think of going over to greet him, but he developed the invisible cocoon or 'force-field' of one long accustomed to abuse.

Apparently, the once lionized celebrity, exploited for political purposes, died alone.

Reading his words, and account of an apparently tragic lifestyle, I found a note of fragile nobility.

I hope that he found the redemption he sought...

A movie described being molested in the school basement during a function – lights turned off suddenly as he was jumped and raped. Lights on to reveal his own father.

Famous playwright raped and molested in England's notorious "Borstal" 'Reform' Schools.

Well known actor raped and battered in private Irish boarding school along with so many others in public and private institutions.

All alcoholics. All in the performing arts.

Why?

At their best, the performing arts explore the human condition, its highs and lows, its exaltations and restorations, the *universality* of our emotive experiences. Once upon a time, it even endorsed a spiritual dimension and even a Christian.

And sadly, often provides more compassion and insight than many clergy.

Even more sadly, has driven away those who could temper those highs and lows with wisdom and the invitation to REDEMPTION.

CHAPTER FIVE

Dynamics – the conflict

The dynamics of the physiology of survival of the body impede the recovery of the mind.

It takes one second to molest a child.

Not much longer to completely destroy a child's innocence and trust.

The child can react with tension and fear, with consequent tissue damage and emotional splitting.

The skilled seducer gets the child to relax with drugs, alcohol, spiked candy, variations on Michael Jackson's "Jesus Juice" – wine in pepsi cola cans given to child actors - grooming, toys, lies, "Play" that becomes inappropriate.

The child is swamped with conflicting emotions that he or she is ill equipped to process and either shuts down emotionally, splits or becomes dependent on the molester.

In adult years, that child will suffer immensely from guilt - probably the cruelest effect of the predator's action.

A male may find comfort in association with other molestees or rape victims, or alcohol, drugs, gambling and other addictive behavior.

The more common female response would be to seek 'punishment' in the form of abusive relationships or sexual promiscuity.

Dissociation

Dissociation is a fancy word for emotional splitting, ie, disharmony of mind, body and emotion. Extreme detachment from sensation, abreaction, fugal states – when the mind becomes 'foggy' and shuts down. Also happens with hypoxia – anemia or environmentally related, hypoglycemia and other conditions. In extreme and prolonged cases of abuse, memories become buried and the personality itself splits. The latter is most common in the case of incest, where the experience is so traumatic, the mind blocks it, the 'memory ions' freeze in 'mid synapse' and the experience is never examined or resolved, until an extreme situation arises, eg, suicide, murder or avoidable accident.

A lesser degree of dissociation occurs in the majority of CSA cases – sexuality can become an end in itself, divorced from the integrated sharing of self with a trusted spouse.

Sexual behavior becomes more risqué and public, aided and abetted by disinhibitors, while the private persona withdraws silently and insidiously, dying internally even as s/he acts out with self-destructive behavior.

Survival

The survivor works through pain and anguish with a trusted, parent, friend, clergy, therapist.

Unfortunately, therapists and social workers subsumed the work of the clergy and created formulaic, legalistic strategies for dealing with deep spiritual wounds.

The goal of contemporary therapy seems to be to get the patient into a "relationship" even while s/he is still working through life threatening issues.

This keeps the patient confused and in continued therapy for years to follow.

Suicidal ideation is common among survivors of Child Sexual Abuse.

A patient recovering from CSA brings his/her confusion to a relationship with another – usually sexually troubled, or addicted person, and the therapist's mortgage gets paid for at least two years till the "house of sand" relationship breaks down, and the therapist has to work a bit harder to get the patient into another potentially failing "relationship."

Two decades ago, gazillions of Americans went into psychotherapy, almost as a rite of passage, with the effect of more broken families, molested, abused and unprotected children than ever before.

This includes the infamous young schoolyard and movie house shooters.

All of whom were seeing psychiatrists.

Thanks, Doc.

You forgot God.

What's God got to do with it?

CHAPTER SIX

Spirituality and Child Abuse

When the Church abdicated its role as guardian of morals and protectors of hearts, minds and souls to the psychiatrists, it forgot the words of the Master.

"Better a millstone be cast around the neck and he be drowned than he destroy the innocence of one of these children....

A *millstone!* Christ the "forgiver" said that – Over two thousand years ago.

We have his opinion on the subject.

And we ignored it – in favor of the sons of Freud.

Freud, the fellow that sold out his female patients for fame and fortune.

Freud the *enabler* of the prosperous, incestuous, paedo-perv.

Freud – who created a whole theory of – yes, folk – *hysteria,* to cover up for the incest of his wealthy patrons, thereby giving permission to millions of misogynist GPs, specialists, shrinks, etc., to abuse and belittle women, destroy our credibility and create a system of denial about our true condition.

HYSTERIA! From 'hyster' – meaning 'womb.' Ergo, women are hysterical, emotional, irrational creatures.

Freud's minor patients were victims of incest.

And Freud knew and Freud covered it up.

Freud also knew that the price of his career was in the suppression of evidence and the discrediting of witnesses, ie, his own patients – women who trusted the sexually addicted, phallocentric coke-head, *to whom they were often referred by their own influential fathers, uncles or other incesters!*

It only took two centuries for the truth to come out and a few muffled comments by academia to persuade us that well, 'psychiatry has moved on from there.'

Seriously?

Moved on, in large part, to the service of despotism and totalitarianism, eg, Ward Four – but that's for another book.

And then there was Jung, an improvement, but muddling through a spiritual minefield, or more correctly a minefield of spirits, most, apparently malevolent. At one time he describes his house as being rather too full of them... (Memories Reflections Dreams)

Jung gave the unconscious mind omnipotence. It was the unconscious mind the selected the Tarot cards, or influenced the Ouija boards.

Too bad he didn't just keep it to himself as he rejected Christ and hurtled toward Eastern Mysticism, drawing a Mandala a day, in order to interpret his own unconscious drives and musings. Not unlike the yogic naval gazing of today, and the self-indulgent use of the therapists couch by such as Woody Allen, whose therapist ignored or failed to heal him of his 'Humbert Humbert' complex and lust for whatever "Lolita" on whom he could lay his neurotic paws.

In the meantime cults and bizarre ideologies rushed in to fill the vacuum, as cult after cult sucked families dry of children, inspiration, love, finances, all with the permission of the Rogerian 'if it feels good it must be good' mentality.

How long will it take for bona fide spiritual leaders to reclaim the place of shrinks as healers of hearts and souls, and are they really interested.

Do they even give it a second thought in their sanitized, safe environments, in the large, lonely mansions frequented by house-keepers and spiders?

Therapy has its place in uncovering dark sorrows, in excavating deep wounds. It has a place in the support that it can and should provide a patient embarking on a journey of emotional healing. It can keep a person on track and functioning during times of trauma, bereavement or other occasions of distress.

However, psychotherapy fired God, and since our *primary relationship* is with our Maker/Creator we will not function well until we return Him into our lives.

The definition of "functioning well" may vary, but those who believe that it equates with amassing huge amounts of wealth often die emotionally isolated, or, through the gift of Grace, actively seeking a last-ditch reconciliation with God.

"Our souls cannot rest – until they rest in Thee" stated the reformed 'rake,' St. Augustine of Hippo whose mature years were spent in a profound relationship with God, and whose Divinely Inspired words resonate through the centuries.

Sometimes a person finds the courage to embark on a hazardous journey through spiritual consolation, direction or guidance. Sometimes the healing process begins with the *desire* to heal or be healed, and the offering of that *desire* at a "Healing" Mass, for the Anointing of the Sick, or, for devoted Catholics, the Sacrament of Reconciliation aka 'a hot shower for the soul.' ©

Other times, the journey of therapy, or self-searching, brings the patient/seeker to a plateau where growth cannot continue without the Spiritual Dimension.

We are mind, body, spirit and soul. The mind and body have their services; the spirit and soul require theirs.

Emotional suffering can be the beginning of a search for that Spiritual Dimension, that reconciliation with the Creator, the beneficent, omniscient Father, or it can lead to displaced rage, where disappointment is directed to "organized religion," and "how can God allow this," or – saddest of all:

"He doesn't exist!"

"Love is not loved" (St. Francis of Assisi) as those deprived of love seek Him in all the wrong places.

The sad and pathological obsession of LGBT activists with acting out the crucifixion or a lurid version of Christ's encounter with Mary Magdalene bears sorry witness to that!

CHAPTER SEVEN

Responses

Parental relationships are vitally important and can, often, make all the difference in a child's recovery.

Possible responses:

1. *Child tells parent. Parent becomes hysterical, calls in police, authorities, frightens child. Child retreats, internalizes blame, shame and fear. The mind can split into a dissociative state whereby sexuality becomes disintegrated from the personality as a whole, manifest by unusual behavior patterns: social isolation, auto-eroticism, multiple personality, fugue states, and increasing attraction toward persons with similar experiences.*

2. *Child tells parent. Parent reassures child, gently discusses sharing information with professionals. Parent takes cues from child, does not impose or bully, ensures that the child incurs no guilt or sense of responsibility for the abuse. Parent seeks counselling for self or*

child. Child heals gradually, moves forward into healthy adult hood.

3. *Worst case – Child suppresses event or is afraid to tell, or threatened with death of parent if the police are informed. Child lights fires or acts out sexually, moves towards an adulthood of promiscuity, "lone wolf" encounters, serial monogamy or polyandry, discarded relationships, drugs, alcohol, suicide.*

Targets

1. Well-bred children trained in compliance and respect for authority. The pedophile relies on these childrens' wish not to disappoint their parents and know from experience that such children would find fighting an adult difficult and conflicting.

2. Children from overly strict or abusive backgrounds, who have no advocacy at home and are probably bullied at school. Predators seek out and recognize the wounded, to paraphrase Simone Weil and move in for the "kill."

3. A recently bereaved child who may be socially or environmentally isolated. *A professional predator would use the distress of such a child to seduce him or her.*

4. Any child in a state of confusion, distress or fear. The promise of an adult "protector" can override the warning signals and instincts of that child.

But who can the child tell about it? Will s/he be blamed for "inviting" the assault?

Threats against the life of a parent are a vivid and well recorded part of the MO/Modus Operandus of too many paedo pervs.

This can keep a child compliant and co-operative for years until puberty, and the long internalized stress converts to anorexia, self-harm, self-mutiliation, suicidal ideations, attempted suicide and suicide.

Or – conversion, compliance, co-operation.

And another predator is ready to destroy another generation of children.

CHAPTER EIGHT

Blame and Shame

"Blame and Shame" are the paedo-pervs best friends.

Parents will automatically assume a sense of guilt and shame for not sufficiently protecting their child – and hopefully re-direct their initial sense of anger, rage and helplessness toward the prosecution of the predator, and not lash out at the child.

The child may expect punishment or blame for "shaming" the family – quite common in Ireland – or accusing an estimable member of the community.

Emotionally "battening down the hatches" and allowing a "friendship" with the predator can be rationalized as a promise of security, safety, social advancement and an end to the fear and confusion of the victim.

Capitulation puts the innocent at high risk of identifying with and becoming the predator-perv.

The child victim will act instinctively, without processing nor having the means to process, the increased fear and confusion that will follow.

A late friend of mine was in his late teens when picked up by two notorious pedo-pervs who ran one of Ireland's eminent theatres.

My friend was a red-blooded heterosexual teenager, but the pervs persuaded him to come to dinner to discuss his new career as Dublin's newest "thespian" and promised to make him a leading man.

Their leading man.

This kid, working the petrol pumps of an inner city, Dublin, gas station, accepted their invitation and was wined, dined and brandied till these two "Virginia Woolfs" succeeded in seducing him and making him the "son" they fantasized about.

He did become a "leading man" but spent the rest of his life in an alcoholic haze and state of sexual confusion and died before he could enjoy the inheritance of a well-known theatre and elegant, if sepulchral home.

He had a great heart and a kind spirit. RIP.

A leading English movie star told my late husband, another actor and survivor of clerical pedo-pervs that he was raped in the cloakroom of his school. The lights were turned off, but when he got away and switched them on, he saw the face of his own father.

He spent his abbreviated life in an alcoholic haze trying to pick up young leading men, ie, continuing the cycle of child sexual abuse.

Theatre provides a tolerant environment for the wounded and traumatized. Statistics of the 70s demonstrated that 95% of actors come from unhappy homes! Now that it is a more stable and accepted career, those stats may have changed. Where theatre excels is its extremes of darkness, as with the foregoing examples, and the other pinnacles of light and illumination of the human condition.

The highest form of theatre is the understanding of the human condition, the resonance of a universal chord.

Professional playwrights and actors worked diligently to bring a human, *humanitarian* dimension to their plots and characters.

Theatre provides a crucible of compassion, an illuminated window into the lives and suffering of survivors of sexual abuse.

It has, however, been degraded into a propaganda forum for "alternative" agendae, for political issues, for 'community' issues and now demonstrates intolerance and ridicule for the standards that keep humanity rocketing back to stability at times of historical peril, that being, the bonds of Faith, of natural Family and Patria.

'Anything goes' becomes *everything is allowed!*

Forever.

In Ireland, particularly, predation is deep and at highest levels; in academia, politics and religious – though cleaning the predators out of religious orders, and profound disillusionment with their new "landlord" class has left them very short of staff and vocations. They do have immensely valuable properties to convert into elegant apartments or lucrative nursing homes, etc., but without much spiritual inquest or outreach. That so many relish the new power of heading "business" Boards suggests the damage done to the Church by "status" or "economic" vocations and the replacement of quality vocations and formation with 'quantity' is ongoing.

CHAPTER NINE

Freeze and please

Mating rituals have a very important to play in the survival of the human species.

Their purpose is not just to arouse mutual interest between male and female, but to generate, stimulate a set of arousal symptoms that are not just for pleasure, but also for the protection of the parties engaged on procreation.

In normal relations, if contact is not invited, not welcome, any expression of interest or even a touch on the hand can alienate the recipient, but in the case of adult survivors of CSA, shut down the normal defence systems immediately.

A traumatic response is triggered, and endorphins start flooding the system in order to protect. Where an outflow of epinephrine - adrenalin would be the expected response if said advances were not pursued, in the person already traumatized by CSA the body and mind are paralysed by naturally occurring opioids - endo-morphines.

They are finally being recognized as playing a role in the depersonalization and dissociation of persons suffering from long term or latent Child Sexual Abuse or rape related PTSD.

The triggers and release protect the child in one respect, but if untreated for too long, backfire and seriously compromise the recovery of the child to adult, as the child confuses physiologic protective reflex with participation and introjects feelings of blame and shame.

For the timid, or well bred child, "fight or flight" is the least likely response to the flood of endorphins flooding an immature endocrinal and neurological system.

Freezing or shutting down normal reactions, and pleasing the predator becomes a survival mode. Later in life, survivors of CSA may avoid dating or other situations where they may be alone with persons gender-linked to their abuser.

Or they may resort to promiscuity in a misguided attempt to regain control of personhood and personal power.

Studies on "nyphomaniacs" in the sixties demonstrated that little pleasure was derived from sexual encounters. Those studies did not investigate the incidence of CSA in the women studied. The encounters were multiple and depersonalized.

Male survivors of CSA, heterosexual and homosexual are also known to engage in dispassionate, faceless encounters with the aid of alcohol and drugs.

Adult survivors of CSA may also react violently or with hostility to 'amorous' advances. More often, however, the response is one of fear and inability to act on his/her feelings. The CSA survivor needs reinforcement of his/her right to say "No!" and to express his/her needs and wishes, and withhold consent in any and all unwelcome sexual encounters, as forcefully as may be necessary.

Today we understand promiscuity as a result of CSA or unwarranted sexual attention or premature sexualisation of a child by a parent or trusted adult.

In Ireland I encountered a nun who was proud to tell me that she "worked with prostitutes."

I mentioned the probability of Child Sexual Abuse and she countered sharply with the statement that:

"Some of them are from very good families…"

I reminded her that "very good families" were often the most effective in concealing CSA.

She did not respond and thereafter greeted me with ice daggers in her eyes.

The "very good families" were probably funding her work, some with clear consciences, others, not.

After all, Sigmund Freud's fame was on the back of the abused children of "very good families," the "hysterical" Frauleins of Vienna!

Virtual Incest

Virtual incest can be almost as destructive as 'hands on' incest. Excessive emphasis on sexual matters, or focus on his/her anatomy can confuse a child who may then seek clarification from an adult or other child, which then leads to disapproval or accusations of 'weirdness,' etc.

This, then, isolates the child from his/her peers, either by peer pressure or parental diktat, and curiosity leads to exposure.

A remarkably untalented young American became an instant celebrity with lucrative endorsements for a highly staged 'reality' show. She is astonishingly ill informed, so much so that audiences began to question whether her ignorance was authentic or feigned as part of the 'doll' image.

The reality of her life, as star of a "reality" show, is that her father controls her career, her marriage, her honeymoon, her productions, and, even her relationship with her husband.

All of the above, highly sexualized.

Much has been invested in her "image," in cultivating the living Barbie Doll idealized by pathetic, lonely males.

Very little has been invested in her mind.

She is, however, the desired icon of the early third millennium: a mane of tousled blonde hair, glacier white teeth, lots of; a surgically sculpted nose, eyes, cheekbones, chin, and apparent, though unconfirmed, enhancement of other body parts.

To make her even more desirable, her IQ has been maintained in the single digits.

"Daddy's" sexualized darling makes millions for both, and as her "manager," he takes a hefty cut. But such fame is fleeting, and there are thousands of other "Barbies" with virtual talent and good lighting, born every day and waiting in line to be the next public victim of "virtual incest."

On a hopeful note, unlike broken victims of incest she brings buckets of green bucks (money) to her therapists and future.

CHAPTER TEN

Trusted figures

One of my most intriguing subjects was the pill popping pediatrician.

During a seminar in Eastern Europe we came across a street performer who appeared to be about eight years old, performing complicated gymnastic manouevres with an adult male. The pediatrician was mesmerized by the lithe young figure in the leotard and completely indifferent to the propriety of her performance. It was a cold, damp day, and she was using the concrete as a spring board for both hand and foot acrobatics – something that the American Actors' Equity forbids for its members.

His fixation reminded me that he married a woman with two pre-pubescent daughters whose gymnastic events he determinedly attended, and, who, apparently, hate his guts.

His interest in the scantily dressed street gymnast may have been purely voyeuristic, but subsequent conduct and suicidal ideations indicated urgent need for psych intervention. He declines on the basis that he'll lose his medical license if they know he's consulting a psychiatrist. So he and his colleagues just pass around the pills.

American Psychiatric Association

Factions within this APA are seeking to 'normalise' pedo "philia."

The same APA that protects members who violate all professional ethics with regard to relationships with adult patients!

The same APA whose members sent pedophile priests, teachers and doctors back into circulation with a 'clean bill of health!'

And of course a fistful of psychotropes, the same pills that make the perpetrator feel euphoric and lose all contact with his/her conscience, inner voice, supper consciousness, common sense – uppers, downers, sedatives, soporifics, hallucinogens, also known as *disinhibitors*.

And of course a prescription for the laxatives necessary to facilitate an overloaded hepatic system...blocked bile duct, blocked liver, blocked eliminations, blocked emotions...

Other unpleasant side effects can be ameliorated by other pills, which overload the endocrinal and neurological systems and shut down the ability of mind and body to process the horrors endured and the horrors inflicted.

There is no disincentive to stop their abuse. Courts scal records – for the 'protection of the child victims' and the "sons of Sigmund," ie, shrinks provide a "laisser passer" or free ride to danger and temptation with their professional notes of "clearance."

Hollywood constantly pokes fun at psychiatry while providing abundant business for the high priced shrinks serving the industry. Hollywood and the British TV "entertainment" industry consistently promotes Child Sexual Abuse, usually under the disguise of exposing the horror of it.

The victim already knows the horror of it! As does the victim's family. They do not benefit from the majority of "fictionalized" movies where children are portrayed as victims, and their victimization filmed as lubriciously as they can get away with.

Or worse, the child "invites" the assault and the poor Child Rapist depicted as the *de facto* victim.

The predators enjoy such movies. It doesn't take much to set them off – a teddy bear, hair ribbon.

It is not attraction; it is not love.

It is a ferocious addiction, fueled by a profound, even diabolical envy of the sweetness and innocence of God's beautiful children.

And there is, the added warped, power dynamic, in controlling and hurting a helpless child.

That it happened to them years past is NO DAMNED EXCUSE!

CHAPTER ELEVEN

Institutional Abuse

As vicious as child abuse is in any environment, the cruelest and most damaging abuse is that inflicted on a child who cannot escape, a child who is trapped in a Boarding School or other Institution, such as the now notorious Artane Boys' Band of Ireland.

The catch-phrase in "liberated" Ireland was "eight hundred years of British Imperialism."

Blame the Brits.

Yet, Ireland, as a nation, has inflicted as much suffering and injustice on her own people as the Brits. Perhaps more.

The Brits were a clear and present 'enemy.' Have a few drinks, hate them, feel better. No conflict.

Irish child molesters were family or respected clergy. Can't drink that away.

Conflict, conflict and more internalized conflict. The victim could not own his/her visceral emotional response to abuse and assault.

It remained buried, festering, destroying self-confidence, temperance, joy.

Ireland did not round up villagers and set them alight, like Cromwell's armies, it is true – and who were equally ruthless and cruel to England's Catholics, moslem style.

Ireland did however, abduct and kidnap thousands of young pregnant or even 'attractive' and 'flirtatious' women, and threw them into slave labor camps. The Church State 'theocracy' – demon-ocracy, more like - stole and sold their babies, profited from their work and kept it all a deep, dark secret.

Ireland is the only country that sent its teenage girls abroad to support their parents and siblings. Often these girls were in unvetted 'service,' working 24/7 for years for little recompense.

Another dark and dirty secret.

Ireland allowed the psychiatric profession to broadly abuse the process of 'sectioning,' in order to silence "trouble makers," ie the battered wives of politicians, their mistresses, underage or 'over the hill,' and threatening to 'tell' - and political opposition.

Cherchez "Pope" Freud of the new religion of the "sanitized," guilt free mind.

Ireland allowed Government inspectors to ignore chronic, epidemic abuses in institutions financed by the State/taxpayer.

This with the consent of parents, clergy and local authorities alike.

Fully backed by the Irish Gardai. (Police)

Parents, clergy and Government

Across the street from the Gate Theater where the notorious Hilton Edwards and Michael McLiammoir aka Son of Big William, seduced generations of young male wannabe actors, was the less notorious, but equally vile Grooms' Hotel.

The same politicians that allowed young girls to be imprisoned for life in cruel and barbaric conditions in Magdalene Laundries, kept Grooms Hotel open after hours to entertain themselves with young girls and boys aspiring to the entertainment industry.

Indeed, the endorsement, the 'phone call' from one of these pols or persons of influence was almost mandatory for membership in Irish Actors' Equity at the time.

At Grooms' you might see a married Minister dangle a nubile young actress on his knee while imbibing imported French champagne – at a time of high unemployment and great austerity in Ireland; or a young teenage boy barely out of short pants whisked upstairs by a politician up from the country for the day – or by a visiting "casting director" or "producer" from another country.

Any Garda who gave these 'after hours' visitors a parking ticket would find himself walking the beat in a lonely country town for the rest of his life.

This decadent lot were the ones who shut up the mothers of their babies and allowed them to be sent abroad to strangers and profited well from the

Magdalene Laundries without one word of censure from the complicit pseudo Catholic Archbishop McQuaid, seen by concerned but silenced priests, dangling the children of politicians on his episcopal knee.

They also assigned aforesaid Gardai to said barbaric laundries to ensure that none of the "hardened criminals" escaped to tell.

The same with victims of professionals; although if there was no "issue" or child from the union, and criminal implications, then it was the psych ward - as with the GP who seduced a 13 year old, then had his psyche friends lock her up when she turned 15 and threatened to tell.

Some compensation has been made to male victims of abusive institutions. Very little, to women.

Then again, those women are too damaged to protest, to advocate, to even function in the world. They do not have an international homosexual lobby to speak for them.

They live in limbo in the *same communities that destroyed their lives, their hopes, dreams, youths, and which stole and sold their children and sold them for profit.*

"We didn't know that was going on."

Germans didn't know that Hitler was murdering Jews?

Germans did know that Hitler was rounding up the disabled and killing them, and Germans protested.

And were killed, tortured or imprisoned or sent to the Russian front.

No one, to my knowledge, ever protested the Magdalene Laundries and the sale of Irish babies.

Even today, the Chief Justice of the Supreme Court of the United States of America is reported to have two children, *illegally adopted from Ireland, but via a third country, ie, Belize.*

And the world is silent.

The climate of self-righteousness, fear, silence, shame and blame that allowed the Magdalene Laundries to exist in towns around Ireland, generated many other institutional vices and crimes.

Institutional vices and crimes which were ignored by Government Inspectors, Institutional vices and crimes quickly covered up by the respective Institutes.

Returning to Ireland some years ago, I was upset to discover that "Lunch served from 12-12.30" meant "Last orders by 2pm," so no lunch!

I was hungry, angry and frustrated, remembering how in Italy an entire restaurant opened after hours to accommodate weary travelers, and I'm afraid self pity won out and tears flowed down my already cold, damp, cheeks.

"Kind" words brought me out of my misery.

"Ah, you're all right! What's the problem, sure you'll be all right!"

Two youths, apparent teenagers, but possibly undersized from malnutrition and cigarettes, were on either side of me. They were uncomfortably close, so I stepped away, a which point, they ran and I knew I had been duped.

Sure enough, my wallet was missing – a wallet containing a precious letter from Mother Teresa!

That was very upsetting. Even more so was the sense that these young men had been exposed to something very *ugly*, the use of "kindness" as a means of *seduction* - into cruelty or abuse.

They were very warped young men.

It appeared that they had been institutionalized in a reform school. When the Kevin Street Gardai showed me the book of local mug shots and asked what I saw, I said:

"Malnutrition, Traumatic Brain Injury, "Fetal Alcohol" Syndrome, stunted growth or "Failure to Thrive, and the long term effects of Institutional Life …" Inevitably, Drugs and Alcohol were also present.

The physical signs of deprivation were far easier to identify and perhaps even treat than the warping of minds and hearts deprived of love, support and opportunity.

The fall out of the evil of centralization.

My wallet and letter from Mother Teresa were eventually restored, miraculously really, but with considerable help from Dublin's Evening Herald.

I don't know where the motorbike messengers serving the Bank of Ireland were raised, but one summer's day as I sat on the wall outside waiting for a friend I was subjected to unprovoked verbal assaults, misogyny, and verbiage highly contemptuous of women.

Said messengers were inner city Dubliners and likely graduates of the same Institutions as the pickpockets in my previous story.

They would be hired through an agency, which would hire on the basis of personal acquaintance, and not the same level of background checks undergone in the USA.

The language represented an unhealthy, misogynistic attitude and was a predictor of violence against women and children – or any apparently vulnerable creature.

CHAPTER TWELVE

Ireland takes care of everyone but her own...

Such is the reputation of Ireland among European émigrés – at least in the time of Frank and Malachy McCourt. In truth, it is stomach churning to watch Ireland's "nouveau riche" socialites focus on Africa, Romania, etc., when Ireland's children and adults are so damaged, and displaced.

U2's Bono is a vivid example of denial-displacement. Successful Americans "give back" to their communities in the form of 'State of the Art' swimming pools, libraries, hospital wings, etc. New York's Jews are dynamically philanthropic.

Bono, on the other hand, bleats on about Africa – a continent receiving trillions in Foreign Aid – while protecting himself from the Irish "riff-raff" with high walls and a massive, custom designed and artistically etched copper gate capable of electrocuting unwanted intruders should the "need" arise.

Ireland's response to unexpected wealth has been to *deny* the Irish that preceded them to a vast, lonely and primitive continent, and built it from the *underground* up into a great nation. From water tunnels, to roads, to bridges, to high rises, the Irish hands were building the USA, and the bodies of lonely Irish émigrés buried on the spot, without consecrated grave or marker, from Sea to Shining Sea!

Irish bodies – or skeletal remains – can still be found at the base of the Brooklyn Bridge.

Still adolescent, Irish émigrés lived in heartbreaking conditions in order to send money back to their parents and siblings in the Old Country.

And the Old Country joined the EU and said "we don't need you any more – we have houses in France and Spain, and have nothing to do with the loyal and faithful "Famine Irish" of America.

Excluded and rejected, the door to their cousins slammed shut by Lyndon Johnson to provide jobs for America's blacks, and increasingly sidelined and subjected to racial abuse, Irish America began to identify with nouveau (Provisional) Sinn Fein, (PSF) an organization of questionable probity.

PSF, Marxist in orientation and origin, cared little for the Irish in America, or Americans of Irish origin, but talked the familiar talk of Famine and "British Oppression" and so on.

Most of Ireland ignored their Irish cousins except when visiting NY or sending thank you notes for coats and other essentials provided by the 'Muricans.'

The post EU Irish were determined not to be associated with their blue collar cousins – "we're not like the 'Oirish' that went before; we're educated."

Not educated enough. The Irish that went before didn't forget their own people.

We forgot them.

We failed them miserably. And continue to do so.

A young American with the map of Ireland on his face and a deep, abiding love for Ireland was deported – for overstaying a visa, even as thousands of Africans and Mid Easterners of questionable character pour into Ireland and register for the dole, in Ireland, then in Germany, Denmark, etc., and are sworn in as citizens. He has been given asylum in Russia.

Having a great time collecting off the 70% European taxes courtesy of Ryan Air's highly subsidized and bare bones services.

While economics are cited as the main rationale for mass Irish emigration up to the 60s, the back-story is equally sinister.

First, to clarify the use of the word 'sinister' in the context of Irish economics.

It's sinister to consider that under the Brits the Irish had the 11th strongest economy in the world and after

Independence the economy tanked. However, those who had, had in abundance, and those who had not, were deprived of even basic necessities – basic necessities and the right to create, develop and market on their own terms. I would say 'lawful,' but the law was obstructive to enterprise.

Even now, Irish insurance agencies only insure one car per person – even if the second car is held abroad.

The system and society of Ireland is formed and created to generate a sense of morbid helplessness and dependency, but that's for another book.

While economics had a role, the émigrés of my acquaintance in NYC were escaping *abuse*.

The famous writers and dramatists.

The well known actors.

The lawyers, doctors, priests and barkeeps.

The maids and waiters.

Those who did not get away in time escaped through alcohol.

Back to sinister economics.

Large families sharing beds.

Children sleeping between mother and father as a form of 'birth control.'

Adolescent males sleeping with younger brothers.

Abuse of vulnerable children by 'authority' figures –
doctors, clergy, teachers...

No recourse, no justice in an elitist driven system.

All carrying their cross, silently, painfully until
provoked, then lashing out at one and all.

Or taking it out on bewildered spouses and helpless
children by physical battery or soul destroying verbal
abuse.

*If this were planned by a despotic or demonic
government, it could not have worked out better.*

The child molested by authorities is permanently
programmed to fear and obey authorities.

The child molested by family is permanently
programmed to trust authorities and view them as
omnipotent, particularly if that child was rescued by
said authority.

Which is why the Church's betrayal was so heinous.

They had the words of Christ: "Suffer the little
children to come unto me." And "Better a millstone
be placed around his neck and he be drowned than he
hurt one hair of a child's head..."

One hair?

There's going to be one hell of an accounting for the
abused children of Ireland and the world.

CHAPTER THIRTEEN

Child Sexual Abuse and Suicide

The memories never fade

At time of writing, the suicide rate of Ireland is 10 per week – that is recorded, at least! Eight men and two women take their lives in Ireland every single week. Add the migration rate of 1,000 working age Irish per week and Genocide Ireland will soon be *"fait accompli."*

We forget the children we failed – forgot that they grow up, and the scars may fail, but seldom disappear.

Sexually abused and physically abused children suffer from Post Traumatic Stress Disorder, and there is abundant evidence to prove that this carries into adulthood, resulting in passive depression, defensive aggression – as in over reaction, unprovoked aggression or self harm, and the extreme of self directed anger or despair - suicide.

To my knowledge there has been no analysis of the background and motivations of Ireland's male suicides. How many had been institutionalized? How many subject to repeated beatings, molestations, sadistic overtures, bullying?

How many had undiagnosed disorders such as dyslexia, dyspraxia, schizophrenia or chronic physical conditions brought on by malnutrition or hypernatremic, high lipid (salt and fat) poverty diets?

It is estimated that 85% of prisoners in England suffer from dyslexia.

The highest ethnic population in those English prisons are Irish. It is reasonable for any health care professional to anticipate that a significant number of those are survivors of sexual abuse or molestation.

This is one group crying out for attention and rehabilitation.

There is saturation child sexual abuse in moslem populations of any ethnicity. It is public and not hidden. There is a high rate of aggression in said population, and moslems comprise the highest single group in the prison population of the UK.

In at least one case, the long term effects of institutional CSA were fatal.

A man died because he could not stand up to the doctor who destroyed him. Said oncologist had all the indicators of cocaine use, very common among professionals in the Tri-State area of NY, NJ and CT.

He spoke with great grandiosity of the "Crowned heads of Europe" that "consulted" him, yet his waiting room was run down and grungy. His sclera were flat and he would disappear for days on end, refusing to respond to his beeper and pages, then show up, flaccid and pale, saying that he was on a "skiing" trip.

Trailing the white powder, that was for certain. No healthy glow on that fellow.

Then there were the concatenations of misdiagnoses, all nicely covered by insurance.

Dr. "Snow" had one advantage over his patient, a lethal advantage.

"Mark" had survived years of sexual abuse and battery in a private, Carmelite boarding school in Ireland.

"The molestations were preferable to the beatings..."

"Mark" was a frail boy, an asthmatic, constantly passing out. Always hungry and underfed. Little sympathy from his tormenters.

His adolescence was fueled by alcohol and the inability to stand up to authority figures or fight his corner. He was talented and successful, but did not grasp the success he truly deserved, international acclaim.

He always backed down or caved and allowed lesser persons to best him, and once the coke-head oncologist performed a digital rectal exam, he could not stand up to him even to save his own life.

He became the eight year old boy in the Superior's office, and the oncologist became the Superior who called the shots and determined whether he would be fed that day.

Or beaten.

The oncologist proceeded to violate every ethical tenet of medicine and to do a great deal of harm in the name of "Mark's" good medical insurance and his own personal need for that expensive white powder.

He systematically destroyed "Mark" with the ready assistance of modern medicine's bells, whistles and other trappings, and billed the insurance provider for every unnecessary, destructive procedure.

When "Mark" finally acquiesced to his family's pleas to leave the hospital, and Dr. Death came to the end of his bed, looking down upon him – in fact, "staring him down," "Mark" backed down and agreed to stay on.

"Mark" is at peace now but his family and children suffered in a different way.

Pro Life anti-euthanists might note that three different attorneys said that if he were younger, his family would have a cut and dried case against "Dr. Death" and the hospital, but as a Senior Citizen, his life had "no value" in America's courts.

"Dr. Death" has retired, and the hospital in question closed down – possibly under the weight of other lawsuits.

"Dr. Death's" billionaire father made generous donations to Harvard, the alma mater of his son.

Indirectly that may have cost the life of an underprivileged kid from the other side of the world and the other side of the tracks – a self made man put to death by a privileged bully, because his right to self defense and affirmation were destroyed in a theocratic Irish boarding school a half century away.

CHAPTER FOURTEEN

The sins of the fathers...transgenerational effects

It doesn't stop there. "The sins of the fathers are visited on the children – for three generations..."

Visiting Yad Vashem, the Museum of the Holocaust in Tel Aviv, I was informed that the children of Holocaust survivors suffer even more than their parents.

On the surface, this might seem strange. Upon investigation and encounters with survivors, it became apparent that childhood memories of stability, warmth, love, mother's chicken soup, faith practices and traditions such as the Family lighting of the Shabbas candles at the start of the Sabbath, sustained them through the cruelty of the camps.

However, their own children could not enjoy the same level of innocence and optimism. Even when the survivors concealed their own personal suffering and experiences from their children, they were exposed to the horrors of the holocaust in school and hence denied the sense of parental omnipotence, and experience of legal and social protection.

The pedophile's victim also loses the sense of parental "omnipotence." And will never feel safe again.

Untreated, trauma brings its abreactions to everything.

In the case of clerical abuse, the Catholic Church becomes the parent who failed o protect the child, even the parent who invited the predator to tea.

The parent-Church may have done everything they thought to be correct and possible to protect the child, but failed to understand the problem, and so betrayed the child.

The predators are practiced, cunning, devious and ruthless.

Survivors of institutional CSA bring their own psychodynamic to work and family. Most live with chronic psychic and physical pain, are unable to experience joy, to relate normally, to trust kindness. Their world is generally narrow-focused, with limited interest, and social isolation can be preferable to the risk of repetition of trauma intrinsic to the fulfillment of obligatory social sharing, expectations and explanations.

The obvious response of "you don't have to talk about your childhood if you don't wish to" is well meant but specious. The act of self-editing requires a level of re-living.

Confrontation with "normal" childhoods more sharply delineates the chilling loneliness and horror of the abusive institutional experience.

Zach was in his fifties, working as a messenger. He carried documents to and from offices across Manhattan and lived in a Mans' residence. Like so many of the men in the residence he was withdrawn and irritable. He was also desperate to change jobs.

I suggested he visit a certain hospital and start volunteering once in a while. That way he would get to know the staff and be in the front line if a paid job came up.

He immediately started to manifest "institutional behavior" marking the chaplain as top dog, patterning on him and attempted to exclude all the long term volunteers from contact with the chaplain.

His conduct became passive aggressive, covertly obnoxious, a complex of survival strategies essential to the survival of a desperate child abandoned to an institution such as New York State's Letchworth Village, an orphanage and crucible of cruelty, sadism, child battery and child sexual abuse.

Letchworth Village needs investigation and compensation for the children of the fifties. If I only had Zach's word for it, his behavior pattern was sufficient corroboration.

"Mark" who died so tragically, had similar, though more refined manifests.

1. *Locate and mark top authority figure (TAF)*

2. *Ingratiation, alienation, exclusion*

3. *Alienate and divide others from TAF*

4. *Become indispensable*

5. *Survive!*

Its cohorts are also found in the corporate and academic worlds, sometimes even more savage. Stakes are higher. Survival plus, all under a veneer of civility and social rules. May suggest why the product of the English Public (elite) School systems function well in the corporate world. Apart from excellent connections and a healthy trust fund, of course.

However, the participants in those worlds chose to join them, and have the option of leaving, albeit with possible financial penalties.

Seldom can the survivors of institutional abuse follow the biblical and Shakespearean dicta "to thine own self be true."

A survivor of long term, institutional CSA is denied his/her very being – his her 'own self.'

For their children, the effects can be even harsher.

"Nuva" met her husband when she was working as a dog walker in England. She was in her teens, he, a minister in his forties.

They married and had one child. After a very flattering courtship it became a loveless marriage with indifference and rejection eroding my very attractive friend's self-confidence. From a strict military family, she went along and did her 'duty' playing the 'good wife.'

She noticed that her husband would never participate at bath time. He refused to see his daughter naked.

When his daughter reached puberty, people started to come forward with accusations of child rape. The police arrived and arrested. Nuva discovered that her 'husband' had a significant history of assaults on children and child sexual abuse. As he was a minister there were lawsuits following his conviction and prison sentence, leaving her with little to live on.

His bathroom evasions started to make sense. She gave him 'credit' for not wanting to abuse his daughter.

However, something happened to the girl; she couldn't take the shame and became a drug addict and runaway.

Her mother went into therapy and found help and a relationship with her therapist – another form of incest – and can barely cope with life and the needs of her now adult child whom she encouraged to have an abortion. Sin begets sin...

The late Brendan Behan, raped in Borstal, went through life drunk.

He had a "minder," here called "Wounded." "Wounded" scared people, including children. One little girl wouldn't go past him unless she could make a large arc away from him.

For some reason, he didn't scare me. I recognized more pain than anger in the man, but was just as happy that the children kept away.

He was another man who went through life drunk, trying to forget his 'cold, mad, feary father' who raped him, threw him into the outhouse and made him eat excrement.

While he would do se*ual favors for Behan, they both maintained drunken heterosexual relationships, Behan having children in Ireland, and according to some in show biz, also the USA.

Another survivor of clerical child sexual abuse was a delightful and charming man, "Thesp," who could not engage in relations with his wife without at least a fifth of scotch. He could not cope with any contingency, disagreement, debate. He could pay his bills and taxes, show up for work and make it to the bar, but not look for an apartment for his family, or bring his wife to the Hospital when she went into labor during dangerous weather.

Paedo perv and drug addicts usually start on a known target by undermining the relationship with mother and close family members. A remark here, an eyebrow raised there, a "do they really understand you" and "just our little secret" all prime the child with alienating mistrust of the persons most inclined and determined to protect him/her.

The grooming continues until the child feels safe with the perv and then it is taken to another level.

"Thesp" continued this tactic with his children to control and alienate them from their mother. This to appease his own personal insecurities and in this, he was aided and abetted by a slew of actresses, many of whom had similar childhood experiences which they also tried to 'drown out' with liquor.

His daughter was badly affected; to go to her mother for help was to betray her father whom she adored. After his death she allowed her life to be taken over by her much older University tutor, a drunk and survivor of CSA.

He became obsessive and controlling of his "Lolita," who eventually escaped with the help of her 'despised' mother.

She then took up with a young man who trolled for prey online, and who chose as role models, a literary predator named "Valmont" (Dangerous Liaisons) and Adrimalech, the Chancellor of the Gates of Hell!

Like her father, this man had been sent to boarding school, albeit at the onset of his teens at the behest of his mother. The boarding school was run by her brother, later known as one of Ireland's more notorious clerical pedo-pervs who molested and bullied all of "Valmont's" classmate, making him a pariah among the victims of his uncle.

It is likely that "Valmont's" mother is also a survivor of her brother's sexual abuse. Despite having two children and a beautiful grandchild, she is cold and dissociative.

Like many victims who lie to themselves that life is alright and 'nothing really happened' – more common in incest than where the attacker is a stranger – she is an untruthful person, presenting herself as more capable than she really is.

She provided no support for the distraught mother abandoned by her son, until the baby grew up a bit and manifest as a charismatic and brilliant child.

Worse than cold and dissociative is the denial that allowed her to witness her 'boyfriend' molesting her grandson and taking no action.

It was disturbing to watch the mother of the little boy gravitate to the people who abused her, seeking the familiarity of more abuse and rejection and then in conflicted despair, take the little boy to live with a dangerous pedo-perv that she had known in High School.

The child's other grandmother risked abuse and put her life at risk to rescue both child and mother, but the brainwashing of what was now an entire chorus of predators, was too intense, and the little boy's mother went back to the abusers - with a lot of help from an array of counsellors, therapists and Child Protective agencies, even a vindictive Family Court 'Commissioner' - all ambitious, aggressive women, who acquired their positions through political donations, the casting couch, or nepotism; all in the service of child abusers and predators.

All with the blood of children on their hands.

Although many would like to view Child Sexual Assault as a 'one time' event, 'get over it,' the damage to the child's endocrinal system, his/her awareness, his/her sense of safety and inviolability is destroyed, too often forever.

This deeply affects the child victim who then starts to perceive the conduct of the pedo-perv as powerful and begins to co-opt that power to him or herself via emulation, or hates and resents it, and often takes out his anger, fear and confusion on the person with whom he feels most safe or loved – his/her bewildered mother or father, or often, grandma.

CHAPTER FIFTEEN

Social attitudes to child sexual abuse

The Hayes Office, Hollywood's office of self censorship, did us both a service, and disservice.

In limiting screen sexual encounters, it forced writers to more deeply examine the complexities of human relationships. That was the service. In coy rock Hudson/Doris Day style, depictions of married life it left many women disillusioned and disappointed. The good overarched the negative.

Nowadays, man meets woman. Jump cut to the bedroom. Porn producers appear to have taken over the industry, and quality, style and content of contemporary movies suffer accordingly.

You can have just so much huffing, puffing and sweaty writhing before it becomes very boring, and film makers then need to up the ante.

Something, different, dangerous, forbidden. Push the envelope, make something risky, edgy for the director's cut.

In other words – bring on the kiddie porn.

But disguise it as social commentary: Taxi Driver. Prince of Tides, Pretty Woman...

Then again, Hollywood's prudery was pure hypocrisy and a brilliant cover for the sexual exploitation that was part of its machine. Hollywood might argue that actors and actresses already came from troubled backgrounds.

No argument, obviously, where mothers dragged their own children into the offices of various pedophile movie moguls. This only makes their exploitation by such all the more despicable.

Hollywood's history is strewn with suicides, self-destructive behavior, Post Abortion Syndrome, beautiful stars turned recluses and other extreme manifests of CSA syndrome.

Dolores Hart walked away from the Hollywood hothouse and became a cloistered nun.

Arguably the healthiest response.

Though competition is fierce in show biz, there is often more compassion and less hypocrisy than in the more predictable professions.

Aside from work and contracts, obviously, actors live for approval, self discovery and the kindness of strangers. So many have been 'stalled' in childhood, by circumstances outside their control – parental divorce, illness, accident, or assault, and remain emotionally vulnerable and easily manipulated children.

They, at least, do not believe that money will compensate for the loss of self-hood, though it certainly can provide comforts.

Applause and affirmation are important to 'lost' children. On stage or off stage or backstage.

"You are OK." "There is nothing wrong with you." "Something very bad was done to you, over which you had no control whatsoever."

Unless you were taught to give the perpetrator a hard kick on the shins, run like the dickens and *tell*.

The diagnosis of Post Traumatic Stress Disorder may be occasionally misused, but when valid, it is purgatory for those who live with over primed stress triggers.

Adult survivors of punitive Irish institutions must receive appropriate support and help if the nation wants a healthy, clean, non-addicted, creative, independent rather than a supine and derivative society.

END OF PART ONE

PART TWO

PROLOGUE

The Catholic Church was shamed, blamed, sued and silenced, its moral authority in the dust, for clerical abuses that mostly occurred twenty or thirty years before the frenzy of malevolence at the turn of the last millennium.

Yes, it was healthier that the abuses of children, morally reprehensible and enduring in consequences, be exposed. Sunlight is a great disinfectant!

What was not healthy was the intent and level of the LAWFARE directed against the Church.

Care and concern for victims; understanding and insight into the cause and effect of Child Sexual Abuse appeared insignificant and unimportant.

What was important was the public flogging and flagrant humiliation of the Catholic Church, her teaching and congregations.

The Church had to be silenced. Why?

Why the media indifference to the implications and effects of Child Sexual Abuse per se?

Where was the love and concern for children and adult survivors of CSA and their families?

Why was making CSA a *"Catholic"* issue more important than investigating and understanding the diabolical hatred of innocence that motivated these crimes?

And why were decades old crimes suddenly thrown in the face of Catholics and the world at large, when 0.1% of clergy were involved?

Pope John XXIII convened Vatican II as a means of "aggiornamento" – opening the windows of the Church and letting the sun shine in.

It worked. And was used against the Church.

Benedict XVI was castigated as the "Rotweiler" for pursuing Child Sexual Abusers and other immorals out of the priesthood.

Didn't make headlines!

And why is the world silent in the face of a massive cult movement that is 100% complicit, through action, silence and ideology, in the rape of children, minors and non moslem females?

And in the face of the growing, well-funded LGBT movement with its high rate of Child Sexual Abusers?

CHAPTER SIXTEEN

Cultural attitides to CSA

Answers to questions posed in the prologue to Part Two may be answered by an examination of:

1. Western attitudes to Islamic paedo-perversion

2. Academic pronouncements on the 'normality' of adult attraction to children

3. Attempts to normalize paedo-perversion by the American Psychiatric Association

4. The status of children in the world today: trafficked, abducted, 'legally' kidnapped by governments for placement in LGBT families; children used as commodities; babies murdered and cannibalized for organs, eyes, etc., in American hospitals.

Islamic Pedo-perversion

The same subgroup of self-righteous liberals who condemned the Catholic Church for abuses that occurred in the distant past and vehemently prosecuted elderly priests to ensure they died in prison, now fawn over islam and invite their 'imams' to spout their sick and destructive attitudes to child rape on major TV channels and cable.

Christ said "...better a millstone be hung about his neck and he be hanged than he injure one hair of a child's head or give scandal to a child..."

And while, yes, some have grievously sinned, the sin is *against* the teaching of the Church.

On the other hand, the founder of islam, an ideology or 'no exit' cult, one Mohammed, lusted for a five year old, went out to the desert, perhaps with some khat or other hallucinogen, and returned to 'marry' the child and molest her until he could 'consummate' the 'nuptials' when she reached the age of nine.

And his followers have continued to rape, molest, kidnap, abduct, enslave, groom, coerce, marry and promote the molestation and rape of infants and children.

It is the nature and teaching of islam, not an aberrant few, but the foundation and core of islam is the promotion and indulgence in every crime that is abhorrent and even so unthinkable that there are no standing, statutory or existing laws against them, because they are beyond the imagination of all but the most depraved westerner.

And the liberal left is silent.

The hypocrisy is resounding.

Where a small percentage of one group assaults children, the entire group and its teaching is mocked, condemned, vilified, ridiculed with impunity in main stream media, academia and 'social' outlets.

However, when an entire group promotes the rape of infants and children, the same vigilante mob is resoundingly silent.

It is easy then to conclude that the issue of most concern to aforesaid main stream media, academia and social pundits was not the care, concern and welfare of children, but the destruction of the one Institution that has, for the most part done more for the care and protection of children than most others combined.

Countries under the vicious rule of islam, on the other hand, are notorious for the provision of 'arab boys' to special guests, eg, politicians and diplomats. Useful for 'leverage.'

Emigres from islamic countries have changed the life, culture and customs of the new host countries, and not for the better.

The grooming and rape of little girls, the bullying and rape of little boys is now epidemic in England and Scotland, in France, Sweden, Denmark, Italy.

The governments of these countries have pretended not to see the devastation of towns, villages and cities once the mosques go up and the moslems move in.

They imprison their own people for bigamy even as they pay foreign moslems to breed with four wives or more. The host nation, the rescue nation then becomes participant and accomplice in its own demise.

They ignore the honor killings, the incestuous marriages arranged between pubescent girls and elderly uncles in Pakistan, etc.

Pedophile rings enlarge and expand, extending into child trafficking, sexual slavery, child pornography and child murder.

Much of this is imported and, initially, funded by the taxpayers of once civilized Western nations, who cannot summon a 'smidgen' of the self-righteous horror against such felonies, not a hint or whisper of the outrage which they once inflicted on mentally ill priests and enabling bishops.

Or even the gravitas appropriate to such a conflagration of values.

In contemporary America and the EU, morals are for sale to the highest bidder.

CHAPTER SEVENTEEN

Academic pronouncements on Child Sexual Abuse

Alleluia! It's NORMAL!

Normal? Says who?

Academics on both sides of the Atlantic, pretty much simultaneously....

http://www.phillymag.com/news/2014/10/06/pedop hilia-not-a-crime-rutgers-margo-kaplan/#disqus_thread

http://www.huffingtonpost.com/2013/11/01/dsm-pedophilia-mental-disorder-paraphilia_n_4184878.html

and from England

http://www.telegraph.co.uk/comment/10948796/Pae dophilia-is-natural-and-normal-for-males.html

So now children are in even more danger – from the professions that should be protecting them.

Primum non nocere - "First do no harm"

Indeed.

The American Psychiatric Association has found a new way for deviants to 'do harm' with clear consciences. Heaven forbid a child rapist have a *conflict* about his/her deviance, seek spiritual help and defund Dr. Feelgood's alimony payments – or flights to the Casbah for 'man-boy' "encounters."

Ray Blanchard is one of the writers on sexual disorders in the American Psychiatric Associations new Diagnostic and Statistical Manual of Mental Disorders. (DSM) The intent is to 'destigmatise' pedophiles who don't 'act on their desires,' i.e. the one in a million!

According to the APA, the changes make:

"...a subtle but crucial difference that makes it possible for an individual to engage in consensual atypical sexual behavior *without inappropriately being labeled with a mental disorder*" APA DSM-5 Paraphilic Disorders Fact Sheet.

Ray Blanchard: "If you take an individual who has a very strong erotic attraction for children, but who has never acted on it, who never would act on it, who agrees that society's prohibition of adult child sexual interactions should be in place, do you want to say this individual has a mental disorder?

YES!

And extend the definition to those who hyper rationalize and enable sexual deviants.

First of all, an individual who "has a strong erotic attraction for children" has a mental disorder to start with – a disorder requiring investigation and treatment.

Secondly, deviants with strong erotic attractions *act on them* 99% of the time.

"Acting on them" includes hiring pornographers and child rapists. Everyone who pays for child pornography is hiring and supporting murderers, rapists, abusers, sadists, torturers of children.

Every single one.

To be classified as a 'disorder,' a person must:

1. ...feel personal distress about their interest, not merely distress resulting from society's disapproval; or

2. ...have a sexual desire or behavior that involves another person's psychological distress, injury, or death, or a desire for sexual behaviors involving unwilling persons or persons unable to give legal consent.

The APA writers not only need a good editor, they also need their collective heads examined! Preferably under an ice cold shower. "Barking mad" just about sums it up!

Seriously? Do they seriously believe the guff they are presenting to the public that the psychopathological desire to sexually abuse children, and the hatred and envy underlying and motivating that abuse is ...*normal?*

"Normal – is that you!"

It's tantamount to saying that rape is sane and healthy if the rapist feels no remorse.

It is, indeed, a tacit acceptance of sociopathy.

And an endorsement of child rape.

Next question.

Cui bono?

Who benefits?

Child rape is the norm in moslem countries. Adult rape and murder, likewise.

Heaven help the hungry person that steals a slice of bread, however.

That is a crime punishable by dismemberment or death.

Wealthy Saudi Wahabis donated millions of petro dollars earned from the West to prestigious Universities and institutions of learning on both sides of the Atlantic, in order to open doors for their protegees.

This was followed by a massive wave of migration to the West by millions of moslems, all adhering to the laws of Sharia and thereby demanding the 'right' to rape babies, toddlers and pre-pubescent girls and boys.

While the numbers were low, few actually 'demanded' their abhorrent and aberrant 'rights.' They just went ahead and did as they pleased with one European community after another.

It appeared as if they had more rights than the indigenous populations.

And now it appears as if the 'sons of Sigmund' are acquiescing to the sick and perverted demands of the hostile colonisers of islam and collaborating in the 'normalisation' of Child Sexual Abuse and the rape of children.

This is one step closer to de-criminalising it.

What is the price of a child's safety?

What is the price of a psychiatrist's ethics?

Of course, to survivors of 'Ward 4,' 'psychiatrists' ethics' is a complete and utter oxymoron.

Did APA officials accept bribes?

Erratum: Did APA officials accept 'donations?'

Did APA officials accept junkets to Dubai? With 'Arab boys' thrown in for entertainment while hidden cameras were whirring?

Or could the APA possibly be so corrupt and drunk with power that they could come up with the new DSM without any external pressure or incentive whatsoever?

Or are they run by a bunch of child rapists?

And are waiting for Uncle Siggy (Freud) to come back from Hell and declare that it was the victims' fault, that they were hysterical and 'wanted to be raped.'

Like every pedo perv. "The child wanted it." "The child made me do it," etc., etc., *ad nauseum.*

CHAPTER EIGHTEEN

More of the usual suspects...

Ray Blanchard shows up again in Toronto, at a U Toronto conference on ...paedo-perversion.

Paedo-perv promoters from English Universities and PIE showed up with the usual 'saw horses' about little boys *wanting* to be raped by adult men. Of course they said 'have sex.'

In my experience with paedo-pervs, they are so warped, damaged and dissociative that they will rationalize, project, displace and even murder to justify their abuse of children.

They either cannot, or choose not, to understand that a child's innocent trust and affection for adults *is not, in no way, no how, no circumstance whatsoever*, an invitation to sex at any level.

Get out the violins! "Oh those poor pedo-pervs!" It's *our* fault those pervs don't "feel good" about their warped and pervy selves!

Essex University picked another 'winner' in Professor Plummer, emeritus professor of sociology and author of "Perspectives on Paedophilia" - as if racist Derek Walcott wasn't enough of a nightmare for the University!

Plummer's take is as follows:

"The isolation, secrecy, guilt and anguish of many paedophiles," he wrote in "Perspectives on Paedophilia," "are not intrinsic to the phenomenon but are derived from *the extreme social repression placed on minorities* ...

It's our fault then. We should care more about the 'feelings' of the child rapist than about the *safety of the child?* And they're supposed to feel *good* about raping a child? How flaming warped is that!

"Paedophiles are told they are the seducers and rapists of children; *they know their experiences are often loving and tender ones.* They are told that children are pure and innocent, devoid of sexuality; *they know both from their own experiences of childhood and from the children they meet that this is not the case." (Italics mine)*

Is Professor Plummer stark, staring, barking mad? A raving lunatic - or another paedo-perv seeking to justify the abuse of children?

There is NOTHING 'LOVING' or 'TENDER' about or in the Rape and Seduction of children.

NOTHING! NADA! NIENTE! NOWT! NICHS! NIX!
The Paedo-perv seeks to control, dominate, injure, wound, distress, destroy and eviscerate the innocence of the child, the heart, soul, and mind - and sometimes the very life of the child. And yes –
children *are* "pure and innocent!"

The fact that the APA continues to refer to child rapists as 'pedophiles' suggests that they are seriously compromised, corrupt, or incredibly stupid. "Philia" is the Greek for 'brotherly love." Duh! Healthy brothers mentor and teach their younger siblings. They *don't rape them.*

In another book, "Male Intergenerational Intimacy," written in 1991, Plummer provides another distasteful morsel: "As homosexuality has become slightly less open to sustained moral panic, the new pariah of 'child molester' has become the latest folk devil," he wrote.

"Many adult paedophiles say that boys actively seek out sex partners ... 'childhood' itself is not a biological given but an historically produced social object."

Again, more flags, suggesting that Plummer's hard drive needs immediate investigation. I wager he has a Tor account, allowing undetectable transmission of pedo-perv material. But Scotland Yard can get around that.

If Scotland Yard has the political will...and backing...

CHILDHOOD *IS* A BIOLOGICAL GIVEN. AND FACT.

INFANCY IS A BIOLOGICAL GIVEN. AND FACT.

PUBERTY AND ADOLESCENCE ARE....etc.

Of course 'adult paedophiles' ie paedo-perverts will say that boys '*actively seek out sex partners...*'

Because paedo-pervs are sex addicts. *They are addicted to the sense of power that their pathetic minds experience by raping and humiliating a little child.*

They are addicted to the adrenalin rush of danger, of indecency.

They are addicted to the sense of power from the testosterone flooding through their damaged endocrinal systems.

They are sadists, taking sick and perverse pleasure in the cruelty of their actions, and demonically delighted in the lies accepted by the trusting public which feeds into their sense of invincibility and power.

Little boys are trusting and lovable. Feed them, hug them, let them go out to play and they are happy little fellows.

Taking that trust, that affection, that innocence and twisting it into 'actively seek(ing) out sexual partners' clearly manifests the moral degeneracy and bankruptcy of the paedo-perv mentality.

And the moral degenerates are increasingly organized.

And with so many families raised by overworked single mothers, little boys will seek out male role models – not for sex, but for friendship, for football, for affirmation, for understanding of 'bloke-yness,' not rape, not brutal victimization, not homosexuality, not paedo-perversion but to learn how to be a gentleman.

There is so much support and empathy for the paedo –perv in the psychiatric community that I am reluctant to garner any more by emphasizing that in my experience and encounters with paedo-pervs, it was quickly established that they themselves were molested or raped in childhood, usually by a family member or trusted associate of the family.

Again, the outcome depends on multiple factors, primarily a warm, loving ear and affirmative, non judgemental, non-condemnatory words.

Those who have no source of solace, are more likely to grow up hardened and inflict the same pain and suffering on other poor children.

The sons of Sigmund want to normalize them, give them the privileges now accorded other 'alternative' groups, LGBTs, Moslems and Blacks and claim that the desire to hurt and damage children is a quirk of nature, a genetic misadventure.

No power there. No hope of approval or support.

And no 'equality!'

CHAPTER NINETEEN

Cambridge Commies raise their ugly heads

Not content with providing England with the most treasonous weasels in modern History via its "Apostles" Club, Cambridge U seems to want to rival Harvard in decadence.

The number one question for me is: how many millions of pounds sterling/dollars does Cambridge accept from Saudi Arabia?

Or has Cambridge fallen to the dark side of decadence, libertinism and demonics?

It has always had a reputation for left wing extremism, and the artist and writers produced by Cambridge, while witty and erudite enough, seem to have an axe to grind against their home country and traditions.

Perhaps because the 'tradition' for so many of them meant being dumped in a Darwinistic, 'Lord of the Flies' boarding school at the age of eight.

Disclaimer: I cannot be 100% objective in this as my late husband was dumped into an Irish Boarding school at the age of eight and suffered terribly from the consequences of abuse and negligence.

I do think it is bizarre that the Headmaster of a prestigious boy's Boarding School would add 'teddy bears' to the list of 'equipment' because, and this is stated publicly, "it helps the younger boys cry themselves to sleep…"

Seems to be an extraordinary disconnect between the idea of comforting little boys and helping them "cry themselves to sleep" and putting them in such a cold, alienating environment in the first place.

And they graduate secretly enraged with 'mummy,' and pre-conditioned to accept all sorts of cognitive disconnects and dissonance – such as pre-conditioning the West to accept the unacceptable.

Some of the more memorable statements at the July 4-5, 2014, Cambridge conference on definitions of Paedo-perversion in the DSM classification code book include:

(Professor Tromovich, Japan)

"Paedophilic interest is natural and normal for human males. AT least a sizeable minority of normal males would like to have sex with children."

"A sizeable *minority?*" "…of *normal* males?"

So if it's a '*minority,*' then how is it …'*normal?*'

And how 'sizeable' must a 'minority' be before cannibalism, rape, murder, arson, and *child rape* is '*normal?*'

Back to the Merck Manual discourse on mental health. If it's outside the norm it's pathological. Right. The vegetarian in the tribe of cannibals is mentally ill. Not the cannibals with kuru. The Nazis are healthy. Dietrich Boehnhoffer is not.

And so on.

No absolute moral standards.

Outside the Judeo Christian ethos, how can there be? Jews and Christians live by the 10 Commandments handed to Moses by God himself.

All enduring moral codes begin and end there. Christ clarified them with the Beatitudes and the Saints, in living lives conforming the highest rules of charity express and teach their power and value.

The Greeks, the Buddhists and others had a glimmer. The Jews 'got it.'

And Cambridge and Harvard, among other 'jewels' of academia, are determined to lose it.

"Liberating the paedophile: a discursive analysis," and "Danger and difference: the stakes of hebephilia."

Hebephilia is the sexual preference for children in early puberty, typically 11 to 14-year-olds.

"Liberate the paedo-perv?" I think NOT!

"The stakes of hebe-perversion?" A stake driven through the 'heart' of the hebe-perv preferably!

No to "liberation!" No to "paedo perversion," no to "hebe" perversion.

Children have a moral right to safety and security.

Because abortion has opened the gates of Hades to the exploitation of children as 'commodity,' spare parts for sick siblings, eyes and organs for the transplant industry, vital cells for the skin care corporations, the abuse of children as accessories for LGBT 'couples,' sexual pets for the hebes and paedos continues apace, *while society, for the most part, is silent.*

When a man like Tom O'Carroll, former head of PIE (Paedoperv Information Exchange) campaigner for legalization of paedo-perversion and guilty of multiple counts of child sex offenses is out in the world, free to spread his poison and attend conferences at Cambridge University, there has to be complicity at very high levels

Apparently he had a great time and felt "relatively popular!"

England and America's leading psychiatrists, take a bow.

Another 'winner' is Graham Powell. Highly respected and working with all sorts of high level English Police Divisions including the Internet Watch Foundation.

No need to ask why the pervs seem to be winning when Powell comes up with quotes like:

"In the public mind, paedophile attention is generally *assumed to be traumatic and to have lasting and wholly deleterious consequences for the victim. The evidence that we have considered here does not support this view ... we need to ask not why are the effects of paedophile action so large, but why so small.*"

Powell did express regret for his statement to England's Sunday Telegraph, by stating that "...the scientific evidence was so poor in 1981, people just didn't realise what was going on...there was a lack of understanding at the academic level."

Really?

So how come I and others 'got it?' How could I write a paper – unpublished – on certain aspects of Child Sexual Abuse in 1985? And these 'great dons' of academia completely miss it?

Aspects which academia *per se* is still nowhere near approaching.

So why didn't they *ask?*

Why didn't they ask to see transcripts of victims' statements?

Photographs of babies' and childrens' tortured bodies? They could have gotten around privacy issues by concealing identities, etc.

If they were interested. If the Wahabi funded zeitgeist was not directed to the 'normalisation' of child rape.

Are these academic 'geniuses' even aware that reading the above line could set the sicker ones off, that they are on hair-triggers of perversion? That almost anything about a child could set the perverted wheels turning?

Obviously not.

The waters get considerably muddied in the matter of ebe-perv desires as the APA – the American Psychiatric Association tries to differentiate between the sexual assault of a nine year old sexual assault of a 10-14 year old.

After 14, however, anything goes?

After a fierce battle within the APA - which produced it - a proposal to include hebe 'philia' as a disorder in the new edition of the manual has been defeated. The proposal arose because puberty in children has started ever earlier in recent decades and as a result, it was argued, current definitions of paedo 'philia' – pre-pubertal sexual attraction – missed out too many young people.

Seriously?

Ray Blanchard, Professor of Psychiatry at the University of Toronto, who led the APA's working group on the subject, said that unless some other way was found of encompassing hebe 'philia' in the new manual, that was "tantamount to stating that the *APA's official position is that the sexual preference for early pubertal children is normal*".

Note: this man, Blanchard, Professor Psychiatry at U. Toronto, is in a position to direct standards of mental health and public opinion.

This begs the question as to who such a man, drooling at the prospect of legalising child rape, could obtain a chair at Toronto, instead of the seizure of his hard drive and a visit from the Sex Crimes Division of the Toronto PD.

Prof Blanchard was in turn criticised by a speaker at the Cambridge conference, Patrick Singy, of Union College, New York, who said hebe 'philia' would be abused as a diagnosis to detain sex offenders as "mentally ill" under US "sexually violent predator" laws even after they had completed their sentences.

Perhaps the most controversial presentation of all was by Philip Tromovitch, a professor at Doshisha University in Japan, who stated in a presentation on The Prevalence of Paedophilia" that *the "majority of men are probably paedophiles and hebephiles" and that "paedophilic interest is normal and natural in human males".* (Italics mine)

O really, Professor Tromovitch? Do you even know the difference between mentoring and seducing?

Time for Japan's Sex Crimes Division to take a long look at your hard drive! By all accounts, Japan's prisons are small, and very uncomfortable for Westerners.

Normal people would see the "Prevalence" of paedo "philes" as a sinister warning. Paedo pervs see it as a means of *normalisation*.

O'Carroll, the former PIE leader, was thrilled, and described on his blog how he joined Prof Tromovitch and a colleague for drinks after the conference. "The conversation flowed most agreeably, along with the drinks and the beautiful River Cam," he said.
It's fair to say the Tromovitch view does not represent majority academic opinion. It's likely, too, that some of the academic protests against the "stigmatisation" of paedophiles are as much a backlash against the harshness of sex offender laws as anything else. Finally, of course, academic inquiry is supposed to question conventional wisdom and to deal rigorously with the evidence, whether or not the conclusions it leads you to are popular.

Even so, there really is now no shortage of evidence about the harm done by child abuse. In the latest frenzy about the crimes of the past, it's worth watching whether we could, in the future, go back to the intellectual climate which allowed them.

CHAPTER TWENTY

And back to the 'progressive' Left.

At its convention in Lüdenscheid in 1985, the Green Party stateorganization in the western state of North Rhine-Westphalia argued that "nonviolent sexuality" between children and adults should generally be allowed, without any age restrictions. "Consensual sexual relations between adults and children must be decriminalized," the "Children and Youth" task force of the Green Party in the southwestern state of Baden-Württemberg wrote in a position paper at about the same time.

At the same time the Left "Internationale" brigades were screaming about clerical abuse, an abomination in the Catholic Church, but enabled and perpetuated by the sons of Sigmund.

What, pray tell, would they describe as *"nonviolent sexuality?"*

Drugged children?

Groped children?

Kneed children? (moslem style)

Inappropriately posed or photographed children?

And, how, pray tell, would these left wing pervs define *"Consensual?"*

And why was this not *widely reported,* outside the Commie "Tageszeitung?"

And why didn't Der Spiegel or Deutschewelt TV pick up on the series of articles titled:

"Ich liebe Knabchen" - "I Love Boys!"

In which perverts were free to describe and promote the joys of raping boys.

Gitti Hentschel was a co-founder and editor of Tageszeitung from 1979 to 1985 and apparently objected to promoting the sexual abuse of children.

One can only wonder why Gitti Hentschel, as a person of obvious means and connections, did not go mainstream with said objections.

And now the Green is the new Red Party, is backtracking heavily on its support for child sexual abuse and the lobbyists who promoted it.

They are now embarking on an enquiry. How many children were destroyed in the *thirty years* it has taken to come up with a commission to "investigate how long and to what extent" pedo-pervs influenced the 'Green is the New Red' Party.

They need look no farther than their MEP, Member of European Pedo-Parliament, depraved commie-anarchist 'green is the new red,' Daniel Cohn Bendit.

I don't know what 'it' he is bending, but Cohn Bendit is certainly *bent!*

Give us credit for some intelligence, Green Party!

Bendit bragged about sex with children in "The Great Bazaar," written by him in 1975, and including accounts of highly inappropriate abuses of children *while working in a kindergarten.* Predictably, he accuses the children of trying to seduce *him...*

Even if that were true and not a figment of a depraved imagination or trumped up excuse, that would make it acceptable?

Was the world insane? A terrorist working in a kindergarten with children is bad enough, but an anarchistic paedo perv "flirting" with children and enticing them to open his flies and 'stroke it' is beyond comprehension.

Unless you remember the Sex, Drugs, "Love" (Sex) "Peace" (Stoned) and *Exploitation* of the 70s!

Mass communication at its most evil:
"Everybody must get stoned..." said the Beatles, or Dylan, and...

Everybody did *get stoned!* Almost everybody, that is.

And, as usual, the innocent suffered.

Party leaders such as Jurgen Trittlin are now seeking a scapegoat, commissioning an independent researcher to identify the duration, scope and persons most responsible for trying to legalize sex with children.

Cohn Bendit spouts the usual anti 'bourgeois' cant as an excuse for his promotion of child rape on French television and tries to retract and rationalize his writings on 'the most beautiful sex' – *with a SIX YEAR OLD GIRL CHILD!* A child he was hired to care for and protect in a far left kindergarten run by nutjobs and perverts.

Despite his vile and disgusting abuse of children and statements, the left still 'honored' terrorist Cohn Bendit with the "Theodor Heuss Prize for bridge-building in Europe." (UK Sunday Telegraph)

And his German constituents elected him to represent them in the European Parliament, another great parody of democracy. Did they learn nothing from that other (National) Socialist, Adolph Hitler?

"Better a millstone be hung about his neck and he be drowned than he scandalize or injure one hair on a child's head," sayeth the Lord Jesus Christ.

He's been right about everything else!

CHAPTER TWENTY ONE

37% of Homosexuals admit to Molesting Children – the other 63% lied?

Who funded this hieronymous bosch fest?"

By the start of the third millennium, it seemed as if most 'educated' or middle class Americans had been 'rogered.'

The connotations of the word roger can be quite dark:

"The Jolly Roger" – pirate flag

"Rogering" – a term for buggery or sodomy in England's upper class boarding school graduates.

And then there's Rogerian psychology. The psychology of 'feel good' sexuality, 'feel good' everything.

Almost as if the totalitarian element lurking in the dark corners of US Federal (European) Government decided to use the carrot of free sex instead of the stick of coercion.

MK Ultra shut down. George Schultz destroyed all records. Or did he?

Yale University participated in bizarre eugenics 'screenings' – selecting certain students, photographing and measuring them every which way.

Hillary Rodham, now Clinton, was one of the participants.

She is currently a leading contender for the Democrat nomination for the US Presidency.

Was Hillary Rodham Clinton a pre-fab, pre-formed MK Ultra'd candidate for the Presidency of the USA way back when?

Her first job was as secretary to the head of the Communist Party of America. It is not clear whether she was fired from that job or left, but she was a disaster in every job she held since then – most disturbingly in her mockery of a nine year old rape victim.

A young woman mocking a child survivor of rape?

Something very unnatural there.

It cannot be coincidence that advocacy for LGBT activity and 'marriage' is strongest at a time when shadowy NGOS like the UN start pushing for depopulation.

The promotion of Birth control, abortion, and non-reproductive relationships is heavily funded and its strongest advocates, attain high levels of government and are socially elevated.

Not too long ago – at least within living memory – such persons would be considered emotionally bankrupt and morally reprehensible social pariahs.

How did we get from happy families to social deconstruction and seizure of happy children for forced adoption by LGBT couples, fully sanctioned in England's Courts of Law, openly supported by the English *Conservative* Minister for Health and tacitly creeping its way across the USA vie LGBT endorsed Family Court Commissioners, such as the nut job in Washington State that caused untold suffering to my grandson.

Despite outcries in the media, and a Facebook page directed to the incompetence, paedo-perv bias of the aforesaid 'nut job' she continues to destroy families with impunity.

Her fellow political appointees in the "Commission for Judicial Conduct" find no errors, nor abuses, nor dishonesty, nor lack of probity in her blatant perjury, bench bullying, refusal to admit substantiated testimony and bias.

America has really fallen down the 'rabbit' hole in this millennium.

Elected Representatives no longer respond to the need and care of the public which elects and pays for them.

Politicians, banks, local and Federal government agencies, theatre, arts, media, etc., fund and support a radical LGBT movement actively promoting child

sexual abuse in education, entertainment, judiciary –
especially Family Courts in certain jurisdictions.

In England, the Minister for Health openly supports
LGBT adoptions, and his website has instructions on
how LGBTs can obtain subsidies.

Meanwhile, *all across England, women and men are
weeping because their children have been
arbitrarily snatched by Social Service Gestapo and
given to LGBT couples, using a very ugly and
frightening term: FORCED ADOPTION.*

Did Gorbachev "tear down that wall" – or did he
extend the Iron Curtain of Communist totalitarianism
across the rest of Europe.

The following stats and information is highly and
formative and come from an open source website
called http://www.jesus-is-savior.com

The webmeisters there are not too fond of Catholics,
and their approach to sin appears militant, rather
than curative, but their material on homosexuality,
pederasty and pedophilia is pretty well sourced, and
their intent is the protection and safety of children, so
credit where it is due.

Their generosity in the use of material is greatly
appreciated and has been most helpful in the
completion of "Child Sexual Abuse."

CHAPTER TWENTY TWO

Frightening Gay Statistics

Too bad Northern Ireland Health Minister, Jim Wells, did not have our Family Research Institute statistics to hand when he said that a child was more likely to be sexually abused by a homosexual adoptive couple than by normal couples. He was hounded out of his office and resigned along with the hopes and expectations of sane Northern Irish families.

And who will dare protect the children of Northern Ireland now?

An estimated 1.6% of Americans are homosexual. This makes them exceptional, and the other 98.4%, the norm.

Hence the term, 'normal.'

By observation, I have noticed that little girls raised by male homosexuals are sexually aware and precocious.

Boys raised by female couples tend to be more withdrawn...

The rate of runaways is higher in children adopted by homosexuals of either gender. The rate of homosexual orientation in young children raised by homosexual parents is staggeringly higher than the norm.

Judith Reisman cites homosexual authors, David Island and Patrick Latellier in her book, "Crafting Gay Bisexual Children." They estimate that, every year, 650,000 homosexual men are battered by a partner. In "Men Who Beat the Men who 'Love' Them," By their count, the rate of homosexual to homosexual violence is three times more than heterosexual to homosexual violence.

Even factoring the percentage of "rough trade" and anonymous encounters, the rate is still very high.

Island and Latellier also estimate that 20% of homosexual relationships are poisoned by domestic violence.

Hardly the image presented in "Will and Grace," "American Beauty," and other such cosmetic, agenda driven show, whether the only health, "slap happy" relationships are those of the 'gay boys' down the hall.

Despite the public

Although most homosexual activists publicly deny that they want access to boys, many homosexual groups around the world are working aggressively to lower the age of sexual consent. Their cause is being aided by the professional psychiatric and psychological associations, which have moved in recent years toward normalizing pedophilia, much as they did with homosexuality in the early 1970s.

Kevin Bishop, an admitted pederast (pedophile), is promoting the work of the North American /Man-Boy Love Association (NAMBLA) in South Africa. Bishop, who was molested at the age of six, is also an admitted homosexual who is blatant about the relationship between homosexuality and pedophilia. "Scratch the average homosexual and you will find a pedophile," said Bishop in an interview with the Electronic Mail & Guardian (June 30, 1997). *(Angella Johnson, "The man who loves to love boys," Electronic Mail & Guardian, June 30, 1997, http://www.mg.co.za/mg.)*

This pedophile/homosexual activist, Kevin Bishop, began studying 'pedophilia' while a student at Rhodes University. He also discovered Karl Marx there, as well as other literature that helped form his worldview. His views are being echoed around the world by homosexual activists who are seeking what they call "sexual freedom" for children.

Bishop is on a crusade in South Africa to have "age of sexual consent laws" abolished, and he is looking for help from NAMBLA to accomplish his goal. He says children must be empowered "by teaching them about loving relationships at an early age, and giving them the opportunity to make an informed decision about having [sex]."

He also approves of incest, noting, "Two women psychologists in America say the healthiest introduction to sex for a child should be with their [sic] parents, because it is less threatening and the emotional intimacy more comfortable." *(Angella Johnson, "The man who loves to love boys," Electronic Mail & Guardian, June 30, 1997, http://www.mg.co.za/mg.)*

Bishop agrees with NAMBLA that the next social movement in Western politics will be an attack m "sexual ageism," which prohibits sexual contact based on age differences. The movement already is well under way in Europe and Canada.

Sexual ageism?

They'll say *anything* to push their agenda.

Homosexuals did not need scientific evidence, neither do pedo pervs.

The public approval of homosexuality and the idea of homosexuals "marrying" would have been unheard of thirty years ago. But the homosexual campaign's success did not depend on rightness or on scientific evidence - but in its image, and on the increasing permissiveness of society. Dr John Money of John Hopkins University has urged pedo-pervs *not to be discouraged by the lack of evidence* backing up their cause. He says:

"When the gay rights activists became politically active, there wasn't a sufficient body of scientific information for them to base their gay activism on. *So, you don't have to have a basic body of scientific information in order to decide to work actively for a particular ideology.* As long as you're prepared to be put in Jail. Isn't that how social change has always taken place?"

This quote comes from the "scholarly" Dutch journal, Paidika — A Journal of pedophilia. "If homosexuality has been posed as healthy, good and normal, in the face of overwhelming evidence to the contrary, so can pedophilia."

Pro-pedophilic articles are making their way into academia.

More like pro pedo-pervs are making their way *out* of academia and into the mainstream.

SOURCE: Africa Christian Action
Book: *The PinkAgenda: Sexual Revolution in South Africa and the Ruin of the Family*
By Christine MC Cafferty with Peter Hammond

PAEDO PERVERSION IN THE USA

Homosexual activists in the USA are more covert about their efforts to gain access to children than in

Canada or Europe. While NAMBLA has regularly marched in homosexual pride parades in New York, San Francisco and other major cities, homosexual activists in the USA publicly disassociate themselves from pedo pervs as part of a public relations strategy.

Despite 73% admitting to sex with minors under the age of 16, homosexual activists in the USA are determined to separate homosexuality from paedo-perversion, preferring to present the sanitised image of mature, professional couples raising a 'family,' ie, someone else's children, together. The truth is much sadder.

Homosexual groups are actively recruiting gay youth through such groups as "The Sexual Minority Youth Assistance League", "The HettrickMartin Institute," AIDS service providers and *various agencies that assist runaways*.

Talk about *predation* - on the lost, lonely, homeless, confused and vulnerable youth of America – the children and grandchildren of the "Love, Peace and Drugs" movement.

"Love, Peace and Drugs" is a misnomer for the Communist led sexual exploitation, bullying and intoxication movement of the 60s, 70s and 80s. It has contaminated three generations, opened the door to the destruction of the family, the disenfranchisement of children as new and 'protected members' of the family and community, and opened the door to social and belligerent invasion by the very cultures that shipped the drugs to our shores, and for whom the rape and murder of little children is the norm.

A determined effort to change age-of-consent laws is under way, first by inuring the public to the concept of under-age marriage and relations. It has some highly intriguing supporters, such as Supreme Court Justice Ruth Bader Ginsberg!

As an attorney for the ACLU, she co-authored a report recommending that *the age of consent for sexual acts be lowered to 12 years of age."*

RUTH BADER GINSBURG WANTS CHILDREN TO HAVE SEX AT THE AGE OF 12.

This promotor of perversion and predation is making enduring decisions affecting the lives of Americans in all 50 States, through devious legal manipulation. So much for 'probity!'

Source: *"Sex Bias in the U.S. Code," Report for the U.S. Commission on Civil Rights, April 1977, p. 102, quoted in "Ruth Bader Ginsburg's Feminist World View," The Phyllis Schlafly Report, Vol. 26, No. 12, Section 1, p.3.*

The paragraph reads as follows: '"Eliminate the phrase "carnal knowledge of any female, not his wife, who has not attained the age of 16 years" and substitute a federal, sex-neutral definition of the offense.... A person is guilty of an offense if he engages in a sexual act with another person.... [and] the other person is, in fact, less than 12 years old..)

The public still has a revulsion against child sexual abuse. In fact, whenever there is an attempt to show a connection between paedo pervs and homosexuality, the standard response from the activists is that as many as 97 percent of all pedo pervs are heterosexuals and/or married men. Thus, they deflect attention away from their own proclivities to have sex with children.

There is some truth to the claim that many pedo 'philes' are heterosexually oriented men. To be accurate, pedo 'philia' is the crime of sexually molesting a child of the opposite sex. Pederasty, on the other hand, is the crime of molesting a child of the same sex. The term pedophile is used as a general term to describe a person who molests any child, and the term pedo 'philia,' however, is commonly used to refer to child sexual abuse in general. The homosexual who molests a child of the same sex, therefore, technically is guilty of *pederasty*, rather than pedophilia - yet both are child sexual abuse.

Again, PHILIA is a complete and utter misnomer and sham.

'Philia' is Greek for 'Brotherly Love.'

There is nothing 'Loving" or 'Brotherly" in the pedo-pervs *desire* to destroy the innocence of a child.

It is so bizarre and hate-filled as to belong in the realm of the demonic.

It can be explained to some degree by 'dissociation.' The pedo-perv lives in a completely different world from the rest of us.

Homosexuals deny that there is a high incidence of child molestation among them, but the statistics tell another story.

First, we need to look at the statistics on child sexual abuse in general. The National Committee to Prevent Child Abuse (NCPCA) has published the following information:

1. Reports of sexual abuse are on the increase in our nation.

2. Between 80 and 95 percent of all child molestation's are committed by men. The NCPCA notes, however, that there is a "dramatic increase in the number of adolescent offenders who have committed sexually aggressive acts against other children."

3. Girls are more likely to be the victims of molestation than boys. Males account for 25 to 35 percent of child sexual abuse victims.4 *(4. "Child Sexual Abuse, "National Committee to Prevent Child Abuse, December 1996, http://www.childabuse.org)*

How prevalent is CSA among homosexuals?

- The Gay Report, published by homosexual researchers Jay and Young in 1979, revealed that 73 percent of homosexuals surveyed had at some time had sex with boys 16 to 19 years of age or younger.

- *5 (5. K. Jay and A. Young, The Gay Report (New York: Summit Books, 1979), p. 275.)*

- Although homosexuals account for less than two percent of the population, they constitute about a third of child molesters.

- *6 (6. K. Freund and R.I. Watson, "The Proportions of Heterosexual and Homosexual Pedophiles Among Sex Offenders Against Children: An Exploratory Study," Journal of Sex and Marital Therapy 18 (Spring 1992): 3443, cited in "The Problem of Pedophilia," op. cit. Also, K. Freund and R.I. Watson, "Pedophilia and Heterosexuality vs. Homosexuality," Journal of Sex and Marital Therapy 10 (Fall 1984): 197, cited in NARTH Fact Sheet.)*

- Further, as noted by the Encino, Calif.-based National Association for research and Therapy of Homosexuality (NARTH), "since homosexual pedophiles victimize far more children than do heterosexual pedophiles, it is estimated that approximately 80 percent or pedophile victims are boys who have been molested by adult males.

- 7 *(7. Thomas Schmidt, Straight and Narrow? Compassion and Clarity in the Homosexuality Debate (Downers Grove, IU: Intervarsity Press), p. 114, cited in "The Problem of Pedophilia, op. cit., p. 2.)*

- A nationwide investigation of child molestation in the Boy Scouts from 1971 to 1991 revealed that more than 2,000 boys reported molestations by adult Scout leaders. (Note: The Scouts, who have 150,000 Scoutmasters and assistant Scoutmasters, ban hundreds of men each year from scouting out of concern that they might abuse boys.)8 *(8. Patrick Boyle, Scout's Honor (Rocklin, Calif.: Prima Publishing, 1994), p. 3l6.)*

- A study of Canadian pedophiles has shown that 30 percent of those studied admitted to having engaged in homosexual acts as adults, and 91 percent of the molesters of non-familial boys admitted to no lifetime sexual contact other than homosexual.

- 9 *(9. W. L. Marshall, et al., "Early onset and deviant sexuality in child molesters," Journal of interpersonal Violence 6 (1991): 323-336, cited in "Pedophilia: The Part of Homosexuality They Don't Want You to see," Colorado for Family Values Report, Vol. 14, March 1994.)*

- Judith A. Reisman, Ph.D., and Charles B. Johnson, Ph.D., conducted a content study of the personal ads in the Advocate, the national gay and lesbian newsmagazine and discovered that "chickens," a common term for underage boys sought for sex, were widely solicited. Many of the advertisements in the magazine solicited boys and teens from within a larger pool of prostitution ads.

- 10 *(10. Judith A. Reisman, Ph.D., "A Content Analysis of 'The Advocate,'" unpublished manuscript p. 18, quoted in "Pedophilia: The Part of Homosexuality They Don't WantYou to See," ibid.)*

- The authors also note a statement from a book review by homosexual activist Larry Kramer that the work, "like much canonized male homosexual literature, involves sexually predatory white men on the prowl for dark-skinned boys to gratify them.

- 11 *(11. From "Lany Kramer's Reading List," The Advocate, January 24, 1995, p. 99, cited in "Status Report," The Reisman & Johnson Report of Partner Solicitation Characteristics as a Reflection of More Sexual Orientation and the Threat to Children, First Principles Press, January 1995.)*

In a 1985 study of the rates of molestation among homosexual pederasts compared to heterosexual pedophiles, Dr. Paul Cameron found the following:

- 153 pederasts had sexually molested 22,981 boys over an average period of 22 years.

- 224 pedophiles had molested 4,435 girls over an average period of 18 years.

- The average pederast molested an average of 150 boys, and each heterosexual pedophile molested an average of 20 girls, a ratio of 7.5 to one.

- 12 *(12. Dr. Paul Cameron, "Homosexual Molestation of Children/Sexual Interaction of Teacher and Pupil," Psychological Reports 57 (1985): 1227-1236.)*

CHAPTER TWENTY THREE

Going after children...

Gaining access to children has been a long-term goal of the homosexual movement. In 1972, the National Coalition of Gay Organizations adopted a 'Gay Rights Platform" that included the following demand: "Repeal of all laws governing the age of sexual consent." David Thorstad, a spokesman for the homosexual rights movement and NAMBLA, clearly states the objectives: 'The ultimate goal of the gay liberation movement is the achievement of sexual freedom for all - not just equal rights for 'lesbians and gay men, but also freedom of sexual expression for young people and children." This goal has not changed since it was articulated in 1972.

Enrique T. Rueda, The Homosexual Network (Old Greenwhich, Connecticut: The Devin Adair Company, 1982), p. 201

In this they have the devious but clear consent of Ruth Bader Ginsberg, Supreme Court Justice of the USA!

Why be surprised. The Supreme Court of the USA licensed, condoned, supported, ratified and legalised the murder of 63 million American babies since 1973, Roe v Wade, which should have been immediately overturned once the testimony was identified as perjurious.

That is almost *one million American citizens murdered every year. Not just the baby, but future generations from that child's lineage.*

How can we turn around and say UN Agenda 21 is a myth and depopulation a 'conspiracy theory' when the most powerful and wealthy people in the nation – and world – put so much heat and muscle in the destruction of life and the promotion of unhealthy, life shortening, non-reproductive relationships.

AGE OF CONSENT

Homosexual organizations around the world have embarked upon a vigorous campaign to lower actual age of consent laws by claiming that current laws are discriminatory against homosexuals. In England, for example, a major push is underway to lower the age of sexual consent for homosexuals to 14! OutRage!, a homosexual organization that operates much like ACT UP in the United States, has been leading the crusade. In a statement published on the Queer Intelligence Service website, OutRage! claims that "under-age queers have rights too. They are some of the most vulnerable members of our community. We have a special responsibility to protect their interests and welfare.

Peter Tatchell, "Why We Want an Age of Consent of 14," Queer Intelligence Service, Agenda for Gay Law Reform, OutRage!, London, Sept. 10, 1998, http://www.OutRage.cygnet.co.uk.

SOURCE: Frank V. York and Robert H. Knight, "Homosexual Activists Work To Normalize Sex with Boys"

ENTER NAMBLA (*NORTH AMERICAN MAN BOY LOVE ASSOCIATION*)

"NAMBLA is nothing more or less than an egregious organization of pedophiles."- Mike Echols in the L.A. Times 3/11/92

According to their website, NAMBLA's goal is to end the extreme oppression of men and boys in mutually consensual relationships by:

- building understanding and support for such relationships;

- educating the general public on the *benevolent* nature of man/boy love;

- cooperating with lesbian, gay, feminist, and other liberation movements;

- supporting the liberation of persons of all ages from sexual prejudice and oppression.

- Their membership is open to everyone sympathetic to man/boy love and personal freedom.

NAMBLA EXPOSED

In 1991 NAMBLA had over 3,000 members. However, that was prior to January 1992 when Mike Echols went to San Francisco's KRON-TV (NBC) and worked with Jon Dann, Greg Lyon, and Craig Franklin of Target 4 News to take a hidden camera and audio wire into NAMBLA's January 4th public meeting in San Francisco's Potrero Hill Public Library. The resulting video and news of this meeting led to the organization's exposure on KRON-TV News... a story which ran for 18 days straight. And this video along with interviews of Echols were featured on CNN and Geraldo Rivera's syndicated tabloid TV show "NOW It Can Be Told." (Read More)

See NAMBLA'S Website

- NAMBLA for Women Article

- NAMBLA and Pedophilia

- ARTICLES ABOUT NAMBLA MEMBERS

- AMAZON.COM AND NAMBLA
  The Beauty of Adolescent Boys by Astrid
  Jackson (For strong stomachs only!

- (More articles from NAMBLA sickos)
  Pederasty and Homosexuality by David
  Thorstad for NAMBLA

NAMBLA is the Sickest Group on Planet Earth!

PEDERAST GAYS IN THE CATHOLIC CHURCH

**Homosexual Activists Want It Both Ways on Boy
Scouts, Catholic Priests**

www.reclaimamerica.org

For the past few months, the Catholic Church has
been hit with charges of scandal. Hundreds of priests
have been accused of having sexual relations with
under-aged boys. Even worse, when some bishops
were notified by concerned parents, they merely
transferred the offending priest to another parish,
where the cycle of abuse was allowed to continue. So
what has caused the sexual abuse within the Roman
Catholic Church?

*(Most of the scandals are decades old and
considerable efforts to protect children are ongoing.
DM)*

"The overwhelming majority [of these cases involve] homosexuals, but the media steers away," the Reverend Richard John Neuhaus, a Catholic scholar, told the Washington Times.

"It is no secret that there has been a certain moral laxity and that a significant number of active homosexuals entered the priesthood in the last 20 or 30 years" said Janet Folger, national director of the CENTER FOR RECLAIMING AMERICA.

Pro-homosexual critics denounced these claims. Mary Louise Cervone, president of Dignity/USA, a group that claims to represent homosexual Catholics, declared, "It has nothing to do with sexual orientation."

She accused conservative Catholics of "trying to make gay priests the scapegoats for decades of sexual abuse."

"It's ridiculous to blame the molestation problem on celibacy, because the vast majority of priests remain true to their vows," said Folger.

"If what those attacking the Catholic Church as a whole are saying is true, then over 98% of priests are doing their jobs by faithfully following Catholic teachings and not abusing these boys."

Folger added, "In other words, the evidence is clear that this is a homosexual problem, not a celibacy problem."

"I find it ironic that those who attack the Catholic Church for not doing enough to protect these vulnerable boys are the same people who attack the Boy Scouts of America for taking steps to prevent this abuse."

It was never about concern for children.

The Media Assault on the Church in the run up to the Third Millennium was tri-fold in motivation:

- **To bankrupt Dioceses and Parishes**

- **To discourage communicants and vocations**

- **To destroy the moral authority of the Catholic Church.**

Well, the 'immoralists' don't read the Bible as a rule, so they missed out on St. Peter's admonitions:

...and the gates of Hell shall not prevail against it.

Personally, however, I wish the Church had done less of the cheek turning 'mea culpas' and taken 'two swords' to confront this diabolical morass full on.

CHAPTER TWENTY FOUR

Open Source Contributions – Jesus-is-Savior and Family Research Institute.

APA ADMITS MISTAKE ABOUT 'PEDOPHILIA'

The APA has attempted to distance itself from its article about pedophilia ever since the APA was exposed by an organization of psychologists and psychiatrists who treat homosexuals. They are The National Association for Research and Therapy of Homosexuality (NARTH).

BAGLY
In November 1999 a gay organization in Boston, BAGLY, offered $25, plus free dinner and subway tokens, to boys who would come to their headquarters and discuss homosexual sex and other issues. The boys were also invited to a free, three-day, lakeside, weekend retreat in New Hampshire with other "boys" up to 25-years-old who are "attracted to or have sex with other men." None of the politicians or media were interested in this story - even though the organization receives money from the state and works closely with the public schools.

BOSTON MAGAZINE

Boston magazine printed a long, "intellectual" history of the North American Man/Boy Love Association in its May 2001 issue. NAMBLA is the organization which practices and promotes sex between men and boys. The magazine wrote about a documentary video that NAMBLA started but didn't finish. The author of the article said, "It was a rare chance to show the world that they [the lovers of boys] weren't nearly as despicable as people made them out to be." NAMBLA has been sued by the parents of Jeffrey Curley, the 10-year-old who was murdered in Newton in 1997 by two homosexuals who had NAMBLA materials in their possession at the time. But Boston magazine continues to be a cheerleader for men like Reardon, who molest boys.
SOURCE: Massnews.com

BOY SCOUTS

The Boy Scouts are an obvious target for molesters, just like honey and bees. Yet, as they try to keep molesters like Christopher Reardon away from their boys, the Scouts are ridiculed and thwarted. Their money has been cut off by many United.
SOURCE: Massnews.com

CONVICTED CHILD MOLESTER LEADS PROTEST AGAINST SCOUTS

John Hemstreet, a former Boy Scout leader, rallied the opposition to the Boy Scouts in Toledo. President of the Toledo chapters of Parents and Friends of

Lesbians and Gays (PFLAG) and Scouting for All, he still considers himself worthy of a Boy Scout leadership position. Hemstreet, a former priest, admits he molested a 10-year-old boy in 1992. He also confesses to being a homosexual.
SOURCE: Massnews.com

NEW STUDY

"We're saddened but not surprised by a recent University of Pennsylvania study that shows widespread exploitation of children for sex," said Traditional Values Chairman Rev. Lou Sheldon today. "The estimated 95% of boys who are sexually exploited by adult men is all the more reason why we oppose the normalization of homosexuality in our culture."

PEDOPHILIA STANDARD ERODING

Chuck Colson in his Today on BreakPoint said, Most Americans view pedophilia as an abomination. But gay activists are now openly advocating it, calling it inter-generational intimacy. As Mary Eberstadt writes in a provocative article in the Weekly Standard (Jan 1-8, 2001), the social consensus against the sexual exploitation of children is apparently eroding.

UNITED NATIONS

Muslim and Catholic states at the United Nations easily overpowered on April 30, 2002 the European supporters of a global homosexual lobby previously suspended as an observer group at the world body because of links to pedophile groups.
SOURCE: washtimes.com

LINKS AND STUDIES

- **Homosexuals Disproportionately Linked to Child Sex Abuse, Study Says**

- **Pedophilia for Progressives**

- **How Pedophiles Operate**

- **It's Official: 'Diversity' Includes Sex-with-Children and Sex-with-Animals**

- **New Report: Pedophilia more common among 'gays'**

- **Homosexuals are much more likely than heterosexuals to have sex with the underaged**

- **Info on current pedophiles and pederasts**

- **New Study Says 95% Of Sexually-Abused Boys Are Molested By Homosexuals**

- **Profile of a child molester**

- **Understanding and Protecting Your Children From Child Molesters and predators**

- **Child Molestation and Homosexuality**

END

Media Ignores Brutal Murder by Homosexuals

Issue Date: March/April 2000

Matthew Shepard has become a poster boy for the homosexual activists thanks to massive media attention. But what about Jesse Dirkhising? In the small town of Rogers, Arkansas, 13-year-old Jesse died a horrible death at the hands of two sodomites and almost nobody heard about it.

After their arrest, one of the men confessed that he sneaked up on the boy from behind, bound and gagged him and sodomized him repeatedly while the other man watched and gave instructions. After taking a break to eat a sandwich, they noticed that Jesse had stopped breathing.

Police chief Tim Keck called the case one of the most brutal he has seen. How strange that this hideous murder committed by homosexuals has been virtually ignored by the news media. The initial investigation of the Matthew Shepard murder listed robbery as the motive. Later it was inflated into a world-famous hate crime against a hapless homosexual. Apparently it is not politically correct to give the same publicity to hideous murders by sodomites.

SOURCE: Media ignoring crimes by homosexuals.

Why does the "mainstream press" condemn the Catholic Church for allowing predatory homosexuals to destroy the lives of boys, while simultaneously condemning the Boy Scouts of America for *not* allowing precisely the same thing in their organization? —SOURCE

The Gay, Lesbian, and Straight Education Network (GLSEN) *EXPOSED!*

Public Employees Teach Teens 'Gay' Sex Techniques (Including Fisting) at GLSEN Conference At Tufts University

GLSEN Fistgate Scandal at Tufts Detailed By
Massachusetts
News: http://www.massnews.com/past_issues/2000/
Schools/fistarc.htm

Parents Rights Coalition Exposes GLSEN's Radical
Agenda:

Homosexual Teacher Group Targets Kindergartners

Fistgate Teachers Knew They Were Violating Trust

http://www.tampabaycoalition.com/files/1018Browa
rdGLSENloses.htm

TVC's Executive Director Takes On GLSEN With Bill
O'Reilly

Queering The Schools: http://www.city-
journal.org/html/13_2_queering_the_schools.html

National Association For Research And Therapy Of
Homosexuality: Activism In The
Schools: http://www.narth.com/menus/schools.html

Crafting Bi/Homosexual
Children: http://www.regent.edu/acad/schlaw/acade
mics/lawreview/articles/14_2Reisman.PDF

Child Molestation And The Homosexual
Movement: http://www.regent.edu/acad/schlaw/aca
demics/lawreview/articles/14_2baldwin.PDF

Homosexuality
Behavior & Pedophilia: http://us2000.org/cfmc/Pedo
philia.pdf

How To Keep Gay Straight Alliance Clubs Out Of Your Child's Life

Critical Analysis Of GLSEN's Same-Sex Marriage Curriculum For
Teens: http://www.drthrockmorton.com/samesexcur.pdf

Please put these banners on your webpage!

God Says Homosexuality is Morally Reprehensible!

Let the truth be known... homosexuality is a menace to society and undermines the moral integrity of a nation. God will not be mocked!

Homosexual lust is not love.

(Paedo-perversion is not love. It is HATRED! Envy!)

In Romans 1:26, God calls such lusts, "vile affections." "Vile" means "morally reprehensible." Homosexual affections are MORALLY REPREHENSIBLE!

If Rosie O'Donnell wants to label Christians like me* as "radical" because we believe the Word of God, then I'm proud to be radical for my Lord. O'Donnell wouldn't be calling Christ-honoring Christians "radical" if it weren't for the compromised, weak, cowardly, carnal, apostate, so-called "Christians" who have become homo-friendly.

Did you know that *Christianity Today* is homosexual-friendly? *Christianity Today* teaches teens that it's "normal" to be confused about sexual feelings, and that "Some same-sex activity or experimentation does not automatically mean that you are gay."

Can you believe what you are reading... this is from *Christianity Today*!!! Why should God have mercy on this wicked nation? I believe God says to men of God today, the same Words He spoke to Jeremiah concerning Israel...

"Therefore pray not thou for this people, neither lift up cry nor prayer for them, neither make intercession to me: for I will not hear thee" (Jeremiah 7:16).

(I admire the take no prisoners strength of Jesus is Savior.com, but it is possible that Christianity Today is reaching out to molested youth, and trying not to polarise them or drive into 'communities' where they will be 'understood' – and turned into 'fresh meat,' further abused and exploited until they feel that there is no turning back and settle for a lonely, abbreviated life. DM)

Comment from webservant* of Jesus-is-Savior.com...

I do NOT condone hatred toward anyone. In fact, the Bible never directs us to hate anyone (not even the Devil). However, the Bible does teach us to hate evil (Psalm 97:10). The Word of God clearly teaches in Romans 1:26-32 that homosexuality is a horrible sin. According to 1st Corinthians 6:9-10, homosexuals will not be allowed into Heaven. For that matter, no unsaved sinners will be allowed into Heaven. The only hope is through the blood of Jesus Christ which washes our sins away (Colossians 1:14). I do NOT seek to be unkind to anyone, but the Word of God is not going to change (Matthew 5:18). Sodomy (the Bible's term for homosexuality) is sinful in God's eyes! If you don't like it, then get mad at God.

I realize that no homosexual wants to hear a Bible-thumper proclaiming the Word of God that homosexuality is a wicked sin... but homosexuality is a sin! To no surprise, homosexuals are now publishing their own perverted Bibles and creating perverted websites, trying to claim that God permits homosexuality. Now we even have Sodomite ministers. Society can't go much lower. The Bible foretold of these wicked people who would change the Word of God into a lie...

"Wherefore God also gave them up to uncleanness through the lusts of their own hearts, to dishonour their own bodies between themselves: Who changed the truth of God into a lie..." —Romans 1:24-25

Have you believed a lie? Please do not be deceived my friend... homosexuality is a wicked sin that will bring the judgment of God upon you. If you are a homosexual, I do not hate you at all. In fact, I care about you very much, which is why I made this webpage. This webpage isn't intended to make you mad or hurt your feelings (although the truth usually does step on people's toes), it is intended to open your eyes to the truth about homosexuality and to enlighten you concerning the solid Biblical warning against those who would commit homosexuality (or any sin).

The proper way for you to deal with your homosexuality is to face it for what it is... sin. Ask God to forgive you and to help deliver you from the sin of homosexuality. Jesus did not come into the world to condemn you, and neither should anyone else; but the Bible does condemn all of us as horrible sinners (Romans 3:10.23). Jesus came to *SAVE SINNERS*, not to condemn anyone (John 3:16-17). I'll close with the beautiful Words of the Saviour spoken to the woman accused of adultery by the hypocritical religious scribes and Pharisees...

"When Jesus had lifted up himself, and saw none but the woman, he said unto her, Woman, where are those thine accusers? hath no man condemned thee? She said, No man, Lord. And Jesus said unto her, Neither do I condemn thee: go, and sin no more." — John 8:10-11

I love you all in the Lord whoever you may be. Jesus Christ wants to forgive and save you, won't you please **TRUST JESUS NOW.**

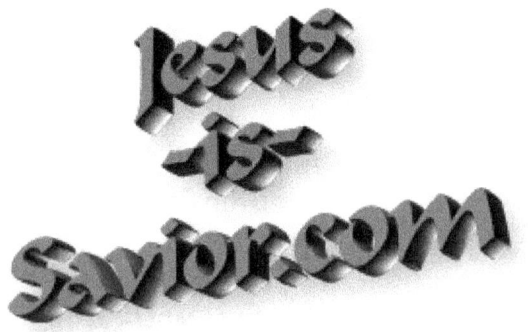

identity disorders. Instead of helping them recover from gender confusion, homosexual teachers consider transgendered teens the new persecuted sexual minority. GLSEN is urging transgender teens to begin lobbying for unisex bathrooms on their campuses.

GLSEN also encouraged homosexual teachers to threaten their schools with lawsuits if school officials refuse to allow GLSEN to start Gay-Straight Alliance (GSA) Clubs on campuses. Not only does GLSEN want a GSA on every campus, they want to violate the rights of parents to keep their children out of such clubs. In one workshop, homosexuals were told that GLSEN is looking for a legal case involving a teen who wants to attend a GSA, but is prevented by his parents from attending. GLSEN will then file a suit against the parents to prevent them from protecting their child from homosexual recruitment. Homosexual teachers obviously believe that children with sexual identity disorders are "their" children-- and that parents have no right to protest homosexual recruitment programs.

What occurred at the GLSEN conference should be a wake-up call to all parents who are concerned about the moral and physical well-being of their children on public school campuses. If GLSEN has its way, parental rights will be a thing of the past. Once free from parental oversight, radical homosexual teachers will indoctrinate a generation of children to embrace a deviant and dangerous sexual lifestyle.

Instead of Gay-Straight Alliance Clubs being run by sexually troubled teens, perhaps it's time for Christian youth leaders to join these clubs to promote morality and the truth about the dangers of homosexuality and promiscuous sexual activities. Sexually confused teens need encouragement to come out of this deadly lifestyle--not to be drawn deeper into a sexual addiction and even death from HIV infection.

(Any Christian youth leader attempting to join such a club would be harassed, persecuted and sued...)

SOURCE: Homosexual Teacher Group Targets Kindergartners

Read what some left-wing sicko public school teacher in California did...

By signing this card, I _____ am taking a stand for a safe and harassment-free school for all students, regardless of sexual orientation or gender identity/expression.

As an ally, I pledge to:

1) Not use anti-LGBT (lesbian, gay, bisexual and transgender) language or slurs
2) Intervene, when I feel I can, in situations where others are using anti-LGBT language or harassing other students
3) Actively support safer schools efforts

_____
(signature)

_____
(date)

GLSEN Learn more online about being an ally at www.glsen.org and www.dayofsilence.org/ally

A California school system refuses to say what action, if any, it will take after it received complaints about a kindergarten teacher who encouraged her students to learn about specifics of homosexuality.

of the bill focuses on hate-crimes reporting, critics point to what they say is "far-reaching language" that will "promote homosexuality and bisexuality to shape the attitudes of

, and countering hatred and intolerance." The bill does not define "hatred" or "intolerance."

Specifically, the bill allows for the appropriation of $150,000 "to contract for the services of an organization with the experience to provide regional training programs throughout the state to assist school district personnel in the identification and determination of hate violence on school campuses, and allocate $2,000,000 for the purpose of providing grants on a competitive basis, as specified, to school districts and county offices of education to enable pupils and teachers to participate in educational programs focused on fostering ethnic sensitivity, overcoming racism and prejudice, and countering hatred and intolerance."

Thomasson said the bill "can easily be used to promote the homosexual agenda to schoolchildren. The bill funds subjective programs that are given carte blanche to deal with 'prejudice,' 'intolerance,' and 'hatred.' This lack of definition is very broad and far-reaching. The funding in the bill can therefore be given to homosexual groups to teach children to approve of homosexuality, bisexuality, transgenderism and transvestitism. There is no clear limit to the 'tolerance' subject matter contained in the bill."

Regarding the bill's funding of tolerance-related "educational programs, Thomasson asks, "Does this mean pro-gay conventions for teachers, such as GLSEN (Gay, Lesbian and Straight Education Network)? Does this mean pro-homosexuality events and field trips for students, such as 'Gay, Lesbian, Bisexual, Transgender and Questioning Youth Lobby Day' at the State Capitol? All these 'programs' are quite possible because of the lack of definition and accountability in the bill."

GLSEN came under fire this year for its "Teach Out" in March, held at Tufts University, which featured Massachusetts Department of Education employees instructing children as young as 14 in how to properly perform homosexual sex acts. It also included a session to help teachers create a pro-homosexual environment in the classroom. The group maintains such conferences are necessary to prevent violence and abuse of homosexual children.

According to its mission statement, "GLSEN creates learning environments that affirm the inherent dignity of all students, and, in so doing, teaches them to respect and accept all of their classmates -- regardless of sexual orientation and gender identity. GLSEN believes that the key to ending anti-gay prejudice and hate-motivated violence is education. And it's for this reason that GLSEN brings together students, educators, families and other community members -- of any sexual orientation -- to reform America's educational system."

Through its self- the next generation of Americans will live in a world without anti-gay prejudice."

But critics believe efforts of groups like GLSEN infringe on their free speech and religious rights. Many religious groups believe the practice of homosexuality is a serious sin and do not want their children taught that it is an acceptable lifestyle. Yet, through the efforts of the Democrat-dominated legislature in California, children are increasingly being taught just that, they complain.

"The pro-homosexual Democrats have imposed much of the homosexual agenda in California. The pro-family community is learning how to fight back. We have much work to do and the battle has just begun," Thomasson said enthusiastically, noting his group's efforts that contributed to the defeat of the November election, giving the party a 50-30 majority in the Assembly and a 26-14 majority in the Senate.

SOURCE: California schools' new homosexual curriculum

END

Child molestation and pedophilia occur far more commonly among homosexuals than among heterosexuals on a per capita basis, according to a new study"

Overwhelming evidence supports the belief that homosexuality is a sexual deviancy often accompanied by disorders that have dire consequences for our culture," wrote Steve Baldwin in, "Child Molestation and the Homosexual Movement," soon to be published by the Regent University Law Review.
Baldwin is the executive director of the Council for National Policy in Washington, D.C.
More

In a survey 68% of people killed in Serial killings were killed by Homosexual serial killers! What is shocking is that Homosexual are only a mere 1.6% of the Population according to the latest DHS Survey!--Heterosexuals are 98.4%! But Homosexuals the mere 1.6% do 68% of the Murders!

Chicago health study reported that the percentage of Chicago AIDS diagnoses connected to homosexual/bisexual men increased from 37% in year 2000 to 44% in 2003; and in mid-2006 it also reported that homosexual/bisexual men accounted for approximately 73% of Chicago syphilis cases

About one-third of homosexuals are infected with active anorectal herpes simplex viruse

Federal Judge Richard Posner envisions Rape licenses!

Homosexuality opens the can of worms for every type of imaginable perversion to be legal—

Once you accept any Perversion the law will not let you pick and chose acceptable perversions.

That would be discrimination!--Liberals do not allow that!

"Cloned robots just following orders" is the end goal of the Liberal depoplationist agenda.

The slippery slope – sliding down the ice mountain straight into the maws of Hell!

Abortion dehumanized the human person. Tiny little babies became 'commodities,' spare parts for siblings or despots.

Children are abandoned and exploited to a degree never considered possible – even in times of war, which left so many homeless and at the mercy of one agency or another.

Now children are kidnapped, by social workers as well as thugs, and placed in danger by social workers – agents of depopulationist governments – as accessories, as playthings, and too often as sexual entertainment by those who promised to care for them.

There is far less follow up on children adopted by LGBT families, then those born naturally to single mothers, yet statistics show such children to be in high risk categories.

Children are the unique and special Smile of God.

www.Jesus-is-Savior.com

Jesus Christ is the ONLY way to Heaven!

With thanks and appreciation to Jesus-Is-Savior.com for generous use of research and other materials.

Disclaimer re the Addendum following:

While I understand that pervs infiltrating the priesthood and living as priests provide a stable population for statistical research, I am concerned that it can re-direct focus toward the priesthood as a cause of pedo perversion, rather than being another target community in which pedo pervs can hide and have access to children.

The focus should be on the pathology and strategies of this most challenging and destructive sexual perversion and addiction.

The statistical research below is complex and thorough, and exclusively by the Family Research Institute, although I have taken the liberty of spacing paragraphs for clarity and italicizing lines that I consider to be particularly pertinent.

I am grateful to Paul Cameron of the Family Research Institute for allowing me to append it, and other information, to "Child Sexual Abuse – Hatred, not Love"

ADDENDUM COURTESY OF THE FAMILY RESEARCH UNIT

By Paul Cameron and Kay Proctor

The Psychiatric Professions Falsely Claim Gays No More Apt to Molest Paul Cameron, Ph.D. and Kay Proctor, M. Ed. Family Research Institute POB 62640, Colorado Springs, CO 80962

Abstract: Although tradition and most hold otherwise, the psychiatric and educational professions assert there is no evidence that male homosexuals are more apt to molest children. Painter's records of U.S. convictions for sodomy 1776-2001 and the John Jay College reports of U.S. Catholic Priest molestations 1950-2010 are examined.

About half (49%) of the sodomy convictions involving homosexuality were of men molesting boys and a disproportionate share (81%) of priest molestations involved boys. If about 22% of priests engage in homosexuality, about 14% (e.g., about a seventh) were caught molesting boys v 1% of heterosexual priests caught molesting girls. Both datasets are discordant with the professions' claim that there is no evidence indicating gays are more apt to molest. © 2012 Paul Cameron & Kay Proctor, Family Research Institute, POB 62640, Colorado Springs, CO 80962 (303) 681.3113 www.familyresearchinst.org

Since Roman times, participants in homosexuality have often been considered contumacious and mendacious. But gays' effect on society – particularly their recruitment of youth – has been a major reason for suppression of homosexuality.

Beliefs that 1) those who enjoy homosexuality seek sex with youth is longstanding (e.g., Aristophanes "lovers of boys" ~300BC) and that 2) they convert the young to their taste is pervasive (Levitt & Klassen, 1974).

Not only was gays' inclination toward boys part of recent professional lore (e.g., McGagy [1971] "homosexual offenders probably constitute about half of molesters who work with children"), but it underpinned formal and informal bars against homosexuals adopting, serving as Scout masters, or teaching school. Tradition considered homosexuality dangerous. It believed males could reasonably-readily acquire homosexual tastes, and those who acquired the fondness would seek to avoid marriage and child rearing – their 'fair share' of creating the future.

Compounding this threat, the homosexually-inclined would seduce others' sons into their proclivity – destroying part of the future contributed by others.

Moore's (1945) "homosexuality is to a very large extent an acquired abnormality and propagates itself as a morally contagious disease," and Halisham's (1956) the "problem of male homosexuality is in essence the problem of the corruption of youth by itself and by its elders" (p. 29) example traditional thought about the mechanism by which homosexual tastes are sustained.

In the US, about 6% of gays v 76% of men are fathers (Cameron & Proctor, 2012). Gays claim sufficient numbers of homosexual virgins to more than make up for this deficit in self-propagation. Thus, in the Cameron & Cameron (1996) dataset, when asked how many virgins they had introduced to homosexuality, the 63 homosexual males who said they had not been homosexually 'married' reported a mean of 3 virgins, the 65 who claimed they had been homosexually 'married' © 2012 Paul Cameron & Kay Proctor, Family Research Institute, POB 62640, Colorado Springs, CO 80962 (303) 681.3113

www.familyresearchinst.org 3 reported a mean of 7 (the means they reported for experience with heterosexual virgins were 0.9 and 0.9 respectively [the 759 married, never divorced heterosexual men reported means of 1.9 heterosexual and 0.04 homosexual virgins]). These findings suggest: 1) some males' sexual tastes are fluid, often encompassing both homo- and heterosexuality; 2) there are insufficient numbers of virgin females to fill heterosexual males' claims; and 3) the average of 5 homosexual virgins/gay is, if at least a quarter 'adopt homosexuality,' sufficient to maintain or expand the gay subculture.

Van Wyk and Geist (1984) noted that boys whose first sexual experience was homosexual were more apt to adopt homosexual tastes. The Cameron and Cameron (1996) study suggested ~60% of males whose first sexual experience was homosexual continued to engage in homosexuality in adulthood whether the experience was consensual (with a peer) or rape (by a man).

It might be argued that Afghanistan and Pakistan are full of homosexually inclined men and demographically stable. Yet that ~15% of their boys are not only sexually exploited, but then consigned to a marginalized existence in adulthood, seems rather a high a price to pay to accommodation male homosexual habits.

Gay researchers (e.g., Kinsey, Pomeroy & Martin, 1948; Jay & Young, 1977) and sympathizers (e.g., Bell & Weinberg, 1978) documented fairly extensive man/boy sex, and Gay Pride parades often include man-boy love groups. Even Evelyn Hooker, the 'gay rights liberator,' opined "theoretical interest in [gays' mental state] is mild compared with concern about the social consequences of homosexuality" (1958, p. 33). In response, gay activists claim they 'are not disproportionately apt to molest' boys and, that even if sex between men and boys occurs, it is not particularly harmful.

Wright & Cummings (2005), long-time members and officers in the American Psychological Association [APA] charge the APA "has chosen ideology over (health) © 2012 Paul Cameron & Kay Proctor, Family Research Institute, POB 62640, Colorado Springs, CO 80962 (303) 681.3113 www.familyresearchinst.org 4 science" in which "advocacy for scientific and professional concerns has been usurped by agenda-driven ideologues...." (xiv), with acceptance of homosexuality being one of its ideologies (e.g., Chapter 4).

Wright & Cummings note "the House of Representatives and the Senate of the United States censured the APA for publishing in one of its journals a meta-analysis and interview study of college students who had been molested as children. The publication challenged the notion that these experiences had been deleterious, setting off a firestorm.., which culminated in the APA being the only professional society in the history of America to be censured by the Congress. ... ...the condemnation was unanimous in both the House and the Senate.

[The APA's 1999 testimony before Congress] "came down heavily on the side of academic freedom and uncensored scientific research and only secondarily against pedophilia.... In private, several members of

Congress confided that the APA testimony was so ambiguous that voting against condemning the APA would have given the appearance of endorsing pedophilia" (xvii) [e.g., appearing to support the notion that even if sex between men and boys occurs, it is not particularly harmful].

Given the then general acceptance of a strong linkage between a man's homosexual interests and sex with boys, it was noteworthy when the APA in 1975 deplored "all public and private discrimination in such areas as employment, housing, public accommodation, and licensing against those who engage in or who have engaged in homosexual activities."

Even more striking was the claim of the APA, the *American Psychiatric Association, and the National Association of Social Workers* in their amicus brief to the U.S. Supreme Court in Romer (1995) that "there is no evidence of any positive correlation between homosexual orientation and child molestation." In Romer the National Education Association, American Federation of Teachers and American Association of University © 2012 Paul Cameron & Kay Proctor, Family Research Institute, POB 62640, Colorado Springs, CO 80962 (303) 681.3113 www.familyresearchinst.org

5 Professors also told the Court that the belief gays "are more likely than heterosexual men to molest children" "is without foundation in fact." (quoted by Cameron, Cameron, & Landess, 1996, p. 385). These assertions countered long-standing belief and

professional lore and ignored the *disproportionate homosexual footprint that has turned up almost wherever child molestation has been explored*. Thus disproportionate homosexual molestation has appeared in generalized studies of child sexual abuse (Able, Becker, Mittleman, Cunningham-Rathner, Roulan, & Murphy, 1987); teacher– pupil sex (Rubin, 1988; Wishnietsky, 1991; Shakeshaft & Cohan, 1995; Cameron & Cameron, 1996; 1998) and sexual abuse by foster and adoptive parents (Cameron, 2005). The APA may have seemed "ambiguous" in 1999 about condemning man-boy sex, but it has been unambiguous in claiming that homosexuality and child molestation are uncorrelated.

When the APA and its allies in the psychiatric-social work professions told the U.S. Supreme Court in 1994 there was no evidence of a linkage of homosexuality and child molestation, *it grossly misrepresented the empirical literature.* Both its 1994 amicus and 1999 testimony before Congress could be seen as "ideology over science." The influence of the changed professional associations' position on the correlation between homosexuality and sex with the underage is widespread.

Thus, in 2011 activists cited the APA's position to legalize homosexuality and homosexual sex with the currently underage in a number of African countries (e.g., Uganda, Ghana, and Cameroon).

Likewise, the then-Presidential-candidate Rick Santorum was criticized by the APA in August, 2011 for dismissing the APA's research on homosexuality as mere opinion rather than science (e.g., "all these associations prove is that they have a point of view and the people who join them, © 2012 Paul Cameron & Kay Proctor, Family Research Institute, POB 62640, Colorado Springs, CO 80962 (303) 681.3113 www.familyresearchinst.org

6 they agree with that point of view. The American Psychological Association is not proof of anything" (Dias, E. September 2, 2011 Time magazine on line). To examine whether the APA's stance is opinion-rather than empirically-driven, two large U.S. on-line datasets are examined: Painter's catalogue of U.S. convictions for sodomy 1776-2001 and U.S. Catholic priest molestations from 1950 to 2010.

Method Sodomy Convictions: George Painter, an openly pro-homosexual legal historian, documented states' sodomy convictions from 1776 through 2001. Giving at least the first few cases of conviction for sodomy in each state, and then highlighting cases as they broke new ground, he referenced, summarized, and commented on many hundreds of convictions (sodomylaws.org/sensibilities /introduction.htm). Painter included enough detail to determine whether the participants were underage in 445 cases (no cases from NH, SD, VT, WV and WY were included because Painter's descriptions for these states were too short or ambiguous to score). We independently scored the remaining 445 cases as being man-man,

man-boy (boy= < age 18), woman-woman, or woman-girl (under the law, 'sodomy' was taken to mean oral sex involving the penis if performed by a male, or involving the vagina whether by a female or male). We had 97% agreement in scoring; disputes were settled by consensus.

We examined Catholic priest molestations in John Jay College of Criminal Justice reports 2004 (http://www.usccb.org/nrb/johnjaystudy/) & Terry, Smith, et al (2011).

As all priests are male, vow to abstain from sex, receive about the same education, and have about the same socioeconomic status, they provide a natural quasi-experimental test of those with homosexual v heterosexual preferences regarding child sexual abuse. © 2012 Paul Cameron & Kay Proctor, Family Research Institute, POB 62640, Colorado Springs, CO 80962 (303) 681.3113 www.familyresearchinst.org

7 Results Convictions for sodomy that included enough detail to determine whether participants were adults or underage from 1776-2001 are summarized by dates in Table 1. With the exception of 37 man-woman and 5 man-girl convictions, the remaining 403 (90.6%) involved homosexual relations. Of convictions for adult homosexuality, 194 (43.6%) involved adult-child events, and 202 (45.4%) adult adult events – *so about 49% of the 396 homosexual convictions involved the underage.*

Generally, state convictions suggest the same pattern. Thus, of states with at least 10 convictions: CA, FL, IL, IN, MD, MI, MO, NY, OH, OK, OR, PA, TX, and WA, there were 130 adult-adult and 125 adult-underage, or 49% of homosexual convictions involved the underage. Proportion of the convictions involving the underage did not appear to systematically vary across the 226 years of Painter's narrative.

Table 1: 445 Convictions for Sodomy 1776-2001

	Man-man	Man-boy	Man-woman	Man-girl	Womanwoman	Boy-boy	Womangirl
1776 – 1872	3	0	0	0	0	0	0
1873 - 1947	46	64	13	4	1	5	0
1948 - 1985	124	117	22	1	1	2	0
1986 - 2001	24	12	2	0	3	0	1
TOTAL	197	193	37	5	5	7	1

Priest Molestations: There are slight discrepancies between the 2004 and 2011 reports' numbers of victims and perpetrators. There were 10,297 (2004) or 10,667 (2011) victims molested by 4,311 (2004) or 4,392 (2011) priests (of 109,694 priests who served during the period, thus conservatively 4,311/109,694 [3.93%] of priests were caught). © 2012 Paul Cameron & Kay Proctor, Family Research Institute, POB 62640, Colorado Springs, CO 80962 (303) 681.3113 www.familyresearchinst.org

8 The 2004 report listed offenders against girls, boys and girls, and boys in Table 3.5.3: 991 priests offended only against girls, 2,805 only against boys, and 157 against both boys and girls (victims' sex was unknown in 429). Dealing with the 3,801 perpetrators whose sex of victim(s) was known,

2,805 + 157 = 2, 962 or 77.9% of the priest offenders engaged in homosexuality (or 'were' homosexual/bisexual). Though some girls might have been molested by an offender who also molested boys but wasn't caught, for estimates we consider 22.1% heterosexual offenders (see Table 2).

Boys were 81% of victims; those aged 9 or under = 1269/8956 = 14% and aged 10-12 = 2970/8956= 33%. Thus, 47% of priests' victims were 30% openness to it (surveys of man-boy sex appear not to have been conducted and published since 1984). If 22% of priests are gay and 13.9% were caught, it would only take 1.5+ more priests to have had sex with boys than were caught to equal 21% (i.e., 20.85%).

21% of caught priests would be roughly in line with the Bell & Weinberg (1978) estimate based on gay self-report. *That 22-23% of gays reported sex with boys – that is, to be a child molester – is to admit to* one of the most disapproved activities in our culture. As such, the actual fraction of gays who have sex with boys is likely higher. From the same © 2012 Paul Cameron & Kay Proctor, Family Research Institute, POB 62640, Colorado Springs, CO 80962 (303) 681.3113 www.familyresearchinst.org

12 perspective, it seems highly improbable that only 4% of priests molested children. Priests almost

always got caught because the children – usually men currently in their 30s and 40s – came forward.

We know that many, perhaps even most, of the homosexually molested never come forward to avoid the stigma of possibly having 'encouraged it' or having been 'corrupted' (see Hall & Hall, 2007). Additionally, given the long period from molestation to being caught in the John Jay study (almost never the same year as the molestation, seldom within 5 years and often 20 to 30 years after the molestation) – it seems likely that many priests didn't get caught.*

Indeed, the accuracy of 'what actually happened?' in the John Jay study is clouded by exceptionally slow reporting: *80.5% of the 10, 667 abuses had occurred by 1985, but only 810 (7.4%) had been reported to the 'registering agency' by 1985*! The media (and legal system) apparently drove reporting -- a third of molestations the dioceses reportedly knew by the end of 2002 were reported-on in 2002 – a year the media focused attention on the phenomenon.

All of the Bell & Weinberg (1978) gays who admitted to sex with boys reported "half or less" of their partners were boys. Likewise, none of the gays in Jay & Young who reported sex with boys under the age of 16 yr. ticked "always" regarding sex with boys and only 1% ticked "very frequently" on the questionnaire. Regarding sex with boys aged 16-19, 2% ticked "always,"6% ticked "very frequently," and 11% "somewhat frequently." These reports scotch the notion that the priest molestations of boys were by 'pedophiles' rather than gays – a point made repeatedly by the John Jay researchers since almost all of the priest victimizers also admitted sex with adults (whose sex was not reported).

That heterosexual priests were so much less apt to be caught strongly suggests they were much less apt to molest the underage (especially as girls are more apt to 'squeal'). As such, the APA claim "there is no evidence of any positive correlation © 2012 Paul Cameron & Kay Proctor, Family Research Institute, POB 62640, Colorado Springs, CO 80962 (303) 681.3113 www.familyresearchinst.org

13 between homosexual orientation and child molestation" as well as the similar claims of the other professional societies' in their amici briefs fail to find support from the John Jay priest data set.

Thus, the contentions of the professional societies about there being no association between child molestation and homosexuality contradict Painter's and the British data sets. *Au contraire, both of these datasets (as well as the US Army study) support the 'older' professional lore regarding disproportionate homosexual molestation of children.*

Weaknesses in these data sets include their unknown degree of representativeness of all sex crime convictions involving the underage, or whether convictions trace a different pattern of victim ages than arrests.

If a professional association that possibly harbors or permits the publication of an unpopular opinion about the harm of man-boy sex is worthy of Congressional censure, *surely falsely testifying to the highest court in the land (and thereby to the world at large) there is 'no evidence' that men with homosexual tastes are more likely to molest boys is worthy of even greater reproach.* © 2012 Paul Cameron & Kay Proctor, Family Research Institute, POB 62640, Colorado Springs, CO 80962 (303) 681.3113 www.familyresearchinst.org 14 References Able GG, Becker JV, Mittleman M, Cunningham-Rathner J, Roulan JL, & Murphy WD. (1987) Self-reported sex crimes of nonincarcerated paraphiliacs. J Interpersonal Violence 2, 3-25. Bell, A. P. & Weinberg, M. S. (1978) Homosexualities: a study of diversity among men and women. New York: Simon & Schuster. Cameron, P. & Cameron, K (1996)

Do homosexual teachers pose a risk to pupils? Journal of Psychology 130, 603-613. Cameron, P. & Cameron, K. (1998)

What proportion of newspaper stories about child molestation involves homosexuality? Psychological Reports 82, 863-871. Cameron, P. (2005) Homosexual Child Molestations by Foster Parents: Illinois, 1997-2002. Psychological Reports 96:227-230. Cameron, P. & Proctor, K. (2012)

Partnered GLBT Die Younger in San Francisco; Married Homosexuals Die Younger In Denmark: GLBT Mentally Disordered? Paper given at Cardinal Wyszynski University, Warsaw, symposium, Gender as the political category, 10/15/2012. Cameron, P., Cameron, K., & Landess, T.

Errors by the American Psychiatric Association, the Psychological Association, and the National Educational Association in representing homosexuality in Amicus Briefs about Amendment 2 to the U.S. Supreme Court. Psychological Reports 1996:79,383-404. Halisham, Q. C. (1956) Homosexuality and society. In Rees, T. and Usill, H.V. They stand apart: a critical survey of the problems of homosexuality. NY: MacMillan, pp. 21-35. Hall RC & Hall RCW (2007)

A profile of pedophilia: definition, characteristics of offenders, recidivism, treatment outcomes, and forensic issues. Mayo Clinic Proceedings, 82(4), 457-471. Hooker, E. (1958)

Male homosexuality in the Rorschach. Journal of Projective Techniques 22, 33-54, p. 33. Jay K & Young A. (1979) The Gay report. N.Y.: Summit. © 2012 Paul Cameron & Kay Proctor, Family Research Institute, POB 62640, Colorado Springs, CO 80962 (303) 681.3113 www.familyresearchinst.org 15 John Jay College, The Nature and Scope of Sexual Abuse of Minors by Catholic Priests and Deacons in the United States, 1950-2002 (Washington, DC: United States Conference of Catholic Bishops, 2004). Kinsey, A. C., Pomeroy, W. B., & Martin, C. E. (1948).

Sexual behavior in the human male. Philadelphia: W.B. Saunders. Levitt, E.E., & Klassen, A.D., Jr. (1974). Public Attitudes toward homosexuality: part of the 1970 national survey by the Institute for Sex Research. Journal of Homosexuality, 1, 29-43. McGagy, C. H. (1971).

Child molesting. Sexual Behavior 1, 16-24. Major Mickle, Dept. of the Army, Homosexual Litigation Update (Feb. 1997), available at http'/dont.stanford.edu/commentary/army.htm (last visited Apr. 2, 2002) Moore, T. V. (1945).

The pathogenesis and treatment of homosexual disorders: A digest of some pertinent evidence. Journal of Personality, 14, 47–83. Plante T. (2010)

Six important points you don't hear about regarding clergy sexual abuse in the Catholic Church: More myths than facts in Catholic clergy sexual abuse discussions Psychology Today March 24. Rubin, S. (1988) Sex education: teachers who sexually abuse students. Paper presented at 24th International Congress of Psychology, Sydney, Australia. Shakeshaft, C. & Cohan, A. (1995)

Sexual abuse of students by school personnel. Phi Delta Kappan 76, 513-520. Terry, K. J., Smith, M.L., Katarina Schuth, K., Kelly, J.R.Vollman, B., Massey, C. (2011)

The Causes and Context of Sexual Abuse of Minors by Catholic Priests in the United States, 1950- 2010. Van Wyk, P.H. & Geist, C.S. (1984).

Psychosexual development of heterosexual, bisexual, and homosexual behavior. Archives of Sexual Behavior, 13, 505-544. Wishnietsky, D. H. (1991) Reported and unreported teacher-student sexual harassment. Journal of Education Researc

Destructive trends in mental health: the well-intentioned path to harm. NY: Taylor & Francis.

*(In the context of contemporary assaults on Christians of all denominations by LGBTs and moslem adherents to child rape, it is equally possible that the decision to report so long ex post facto was strategically encouraged, as in Ireland, and the suffering of the victim exploited by the liberal left to attack and economically cripple the Church.

It would appear that care and concern for children and the long term consequences of Child Sexual Abuse are the last considerations of the self-righteous Church bashing liberals. DM)

FINIS

For further information and resources, Jesus is Savior is a deep and generous wellspring of knowledge and information.

As follows:

Do Something About the Homosexual Movement and Pedophilia!

_____

Gay Marriage is a Sin!

God Loves People (All people!)

Sodomy (Audio sermon by Pastor Jeff Owens)

Hope for Homosexuals | Myths About Homosexuality

The Homosexual Lifestyle is No White Picket Fence

Reclaiming the Rainbow | Sodomite Ministers | Protest Gay Day!

PHILLIES LOSE; REPENT AMERICA WINS

MILITANT MOB OF HOMOSEXUALS TARGET REPENT AMERICA

Education secretary blasts PBS for cartoon with gay characters

George Bush Cheers Gay Church! | High Court to Give 'Gays' Their Own 'Roe'?

Gay Pride? | Gay Tolerance? | Was King James a Homosexual?

While homosexuals claim they make up 10% of the population, the reality is closer to 1-2%

Homosexuality 101: A Primer (.PDF) (Provides a brief history of the homosexual movement in the U.S. and its roots in Marxist ideology. This paper describes how homosexuals terrorized the psychiatric community and have created a marketing strategy to vilify their opponents.)

Homosexuals Recruit Public School Children (.PDF)

Homosexual Behavior Fuels AIDS and STD Epidemic (.PDF)

A Gender Identity Disorder Goes Mainstream (.PDF)

Homosexual Propaganda Campaign Based on Hitler's "Big Lie" Technique (.PDF)

Homosexual Sex = Death from HIV Infection (.PDF)

Traditional Values Coalition Exposes Homosexual Agenda (.PDF)

There is a way out!

If you really love someone, you'll tell them the truth.

For the most wonderful, blessed and beautiful little angel on planet "Earf." May the Lord keep you safe and happy

June 21, 2015

www.ingramcontent.com/pod-product-compliance
Lightning Source LLC
Chambersburg PA
CBHW070909290526
45795CB00001B/257